liberating
NATURE

Theology and Economics
in a New Order

PAUL G. KING AND DAVID O. WOODYARD

The Pilgrim Press
Cleveland, Ohio

The Pilgrim Press, Cleveland, Ohio 44115

© 1999 by Paul G. King and David O. Woodyard

Biblical quotations are from the New Revised Standard Version of the Bible, © 1989 by the Division of Christian Education of the National Council of the Churches of Christ in the U.S.A., and are used by permission

Printed in the United States of America on acid-free paper

04   03   02   01   00   99   5   4   3   2   1

Library of Congress Cataloging-in-Publication Data

King, Paul G., 1940–
    Liberating nature : theology and economics in a new order / Paul G. King and David O. Woodyard.
        p.   cm.
    Includes bibliographical references and index.
    ISBN 0-8298-1317-9 (pbk. : alk. paper)
    1. Economics—Religious aspects—Christianity.   2. Human ecology—Religious aspects—Christianity.   I. Woodyard, David O.
    II. Title.
    BR115.E3K45   1999
    261.8'5—dc21   98-45512
                                                              CIP

To

Donald W. Shriver Jr.,

who has been our mentor,

and our children,

who have become our mentors

·CONTENTS·

·FOREWORD·

John B. Cobb Jr.

In the late 1960s two movements arose with potential to revolutionize the thought and self-understanding of the late twentieth century. One was liberation theology, which provided an understanding of Christian faith that has empowered millions to understand their cry for justice as the place where God is active. The other was the ecological movement, which challenged the narrow anthropocentrism of modernity.

Liberation theology arose in Latin America. It named the treatment of peasants and workers there as oppression and pointed out that much of the biblical message is a protest against such oppression. It analyzed the oppression primarily in terms of class structures and called for overturning these structures.

The civil rights movement of Martin Luther King Jr. developed into more radical calls for the liberation of African Americans in the United States. This movement was given expression in Christian circles by black theology. During the same period, women pointed out the patriarchal structure of society and their age-old domination by men. Within the church, feminist theology arose.

Liberation theology is by its nature particular. It arises in specific contexts of oppression, names the oppression, and shows that the protest against it is continuous with the biblical witness. God is on the side of the oppressed in their struggle for liberation. The particularity gives intensity to the belief and concreteness to the resulting practice, but it limits the direct theoretical relevance. Nevertheless, working alliances have been built among the various liberation struggles, with the result that they can also be seen as many expressions of a single protest against a system of domination.

The ecological movement, in contrast, arose chiefly in middle-class North America, with sister movements in other developed countries. It expressed revulsion for a society so committed to profits and consumption that it refused to notice that its practices were degrading the earth. It pointed to catastrophes ahead if, collectively, we did not learn to preserve rivers and forests and topsoil, avoid polluting air and water, and share the world with other creatures. Although the ecological movement arose outside the church and often viewed the church as an enemy, there was resonance among Christians. Within the church, ecological theology developed alongside liberation theology.

The tendency in both movements to see the other as a competitor distracted attention from what is most important. Some liberation theologians viewed the ecological movement as too narrowly focused on losses in sightseeing and outdoor recreation, while ignoring the terrible suffering of the poor and oppressed. Some in the ecological movement saw liberationists as being concerned about the redistribution of power and wealth on a sinking ship.

Others on both sides were more open to each other. Especially in the church, those who took the ecological crisis seriously were concerned for the well-being of the poor as well. The typical language was that of ecojustice.

Some feminists from the beginning appreciated the importance of the earth. For them, liberation from patriarchy was at once liberation of women and liberation of the earth. Ecofeminism has combined the motifs of liberation and ecology.

Other liberationists have been slower to appreciate the importance of the concerns raised by ecologists. But change has occurred here as well. Ecological concerns, instead of being rejected as those of the rich and powerful, have been added to the list of concerns of the poor and oppressed.

Paul King and David Woodyard approach the issue from the side of liberation theology. They have come to take the ecological crisis with full seriousness. They see that the oppression directed against so many human beings is directed also against the other creatures with whom we share this planet. Without in any way departing from their human liberationist commitments, they are committed to extending these to the liberation of nature. Their work will make it still more difficult for those who want to preserve the present system to play liberationists and ecologists off against each other, especially in the church. It will support the trend, at least since the NGO meeting at the Earth Summit in Rio de Janeiro, for those who seek the health of the earth and those who care about the oppressed to work together and give common expression to their commitments.

This is in itself an important contribution. But there is more. Both liberationists and ecologists are realizing with increasing clarity that it is the economic system, supported by the dominant economic theory, that generates much of the oppression and exploitation we oppose. But it is difficult for those of us who are not educated in the field of economics to assert ourselves with confidence, and we face a formidable consensus on the part of economists who support the present global economic system.

In many ways economists have become the "theologians" of our world. Because the aim of society, and of so many individuals within it, is now defined primarily in economic terms, economists are the ones who guide us and provide the theory that informs their guidance. Most people, if they look to Christian theologians at all, do so for quite limited purposes.

One of the authors of this book is an economist whose understanding of his own discipline is informed by Christian faith. Furthermore, this faith commits him both to human liberation and to the extension of that liberation to other creatures and the earth. The book highlights the features of the current economic consensus that require change if the discipline of economics as a whole is to shift from posing obstacles to liberation to giving it support. Without this kind of guidance from committed economists, the church will lack the confidence to speak or act in this crucial realm. The authors propose actions for the church to take that should be considered with real seriousness.

Of course, the authors' goal is to change the wider society, not just the church. Changes in economic theory must be integrated into actual changes in the ordering of society and its economic arrangement. Without this integration, our theological talk of liberation and of the integrity of creation remains just that.

·PREFACE·

This book, while growing out of the classroom, is written to be accessible and convincing in the living room. When the fate of the public square is at issue, its inhabitants deserve access to understandable literature. In matters ecological, all persons need to be persuaded that nature deserves a presence at the table as our common future is envisioned.

Over the last few years we have tested our work in professional arenas. The critiques of many have drawn our attention to vulnerabilities in our analysis. At an early stage, the critiques of Drs. Ian Barbour and Nancy R. Howell provoked us to rethink parts of our argument. Dr. Herman Daly read the first draft of the manuscript and invited us to reconsider some of what we were doing. Dr. Kent Maynard, our collaborator in a previous work, offered a rigorous critique of the manuscript in its entirety. In the late stages of writing, Kelly Brown Douglas identified themes touched on but inadequately developed. The support of our work over the years by Donald W. Shriver Jr. has been indispensable. We name each with gratitude but without any hints of responsibility for the finished project.

We wish to thank The Pilgrim Press for the rapidity with which it has worked to help us move into the public forum.

We have taught together for over two decades and this book is our third collaboration. Few understand what common themes a theologian and an economist would find to talk about, much less translate into manuscripts. While some of that remains a mystery to us, at the center is a recognition that life is interdisciplinary both as lived and examined. When one adds to that mutual respect as persons and scholars, the mystery recedes to the margin and remains as a reminder of those things most precious in life.

O·N·E

The Origins of Environmental Degradation

When one arrives at the center of our college town on State Route 37, the first thing that may catch one's attention is the churches on the four corners. Granville, Ohio, population 6,800, is a transplanted New England village, settled by adventuresome spirits from Granville, Massachusetts. New Englanders had a tradition of marking off the center of a township and locating the houses of worship there. Visitors to the community, often prospective college students and their parents, typically note the serenity of the setting. It has the feel of a sanctuary; Granville appears somewhat virgin in relation to the evils of the age. At midcentury, a preacher from the East gave one of his first sermons on the doctrine of sin at the Baptist church. Afterwards a deacon said, "It was a lovely sermon, Mr. Kruener. But you need to know, we don't have any sin in Granville." At some symbolic level, that is believable. We appear to be a throwback to a more innocent and uncomplicated time.

For the two of us, arriving in the community as faculty members in the 1960s, it seemed a wonderful, bucolic setting. Everything was green and fresh; there was no unsightly industry; a "traffic jam" meant we had to wait thirty seconds at one of the six traffic lights in town. It was a safe place for us to work and walk, for our children to play. Even when we became aware of pollution in the 1960s, it was something that happened elsewhere, not in Granville.

On the surface, then, it is an unlikely setting in which to consider the intersection of religion and economics with the environment. It is not unlikely in a college classroom, of course, where reality is often imported. Yet it is in this venue, our college town, where this economist and this theologian join others who gather signatures on a petition to arrest development at the community's perimeter, an area coveted by fast-food restaurants, modest motels, gas stations, and sundry other enterprises.

1

Entering Granville from the west on Cherry Street, one has to be perceptive to note the area fenced off with barbed wire and the sign that reads "Warning: Environmental Work in Progress." One's sense of the setting's innocence soon evaporates if one is curious enough to enter the village hall and raise probing questions. The village manager, or perhaps the mayor, can tell the story of how and why the Superfund invested two million dollars in the community. There was a small family business that had for decades operated a chemical recycling and disposal business and that planted chemical waste in tubes in the willing soil. In time, the carcinogenic contents gravitated toward the village water supply. A remedy was beyond the means of the now-defunct business or the small community; as a result, even those who often castigate big government welcomed federal intervention.

In our classroom, we teach about the intersection of religion, economics, and the environment; but they converge in our small village as well. The churches, Wendy's, and the EPA are all a part of our landscape. Even Granville, the place we thought so beautiful and untouched, has played out its own version of "Paradise Lost." We have spent virtually all of our professional lives in this place, and we care passionately about its destiny. That is why, as we worship in two of its churches, resist the incursion of excessive commercial development, and contemplate the brain cancers that have killed three of our colleagues in the last ten years, more than a bit of anger eclipses both our own security and the seeming serenity of the setting.

Anger is not usually thought to be a virtue; love is much to be preferred. But, at least in this case, love without anger is much like righteousness without wrath. It isn't going to do much about what is wrong. Passion is not evil and emotion is not the antithesis of rationality. Just as passionate commitment may drive reason to a more meaningful embrace with reality, so too anger can be the servant of a morality driven by love. After all, Jesus did drive the money changers out of the temple. As Beverly Harrison writes, "Anger is a *mode of connectedness* to others and it is always a *vivid form of caring*."[1] And the two of us, an economist and a theologian, exercise our love for our community by expressing our anger through participation in a citizens' revolt. Religion, economics, and the environment are in our classroom to be sure; but even more vividly they define the reality of our common life in Granville, Ohio.

We did not arrive at this recognition directly or easily. Our professional collaboration has now spanned three books and eighteen years. In the first book, we were exploring whether liberation theology and economics might have anything useful to say to each other in the context of social change. We answered in the affirmative. But when we looked back at that work a few years later, we realized that, for us, it had become necessary not just to connect the two disciplines, but to position our analysis in relation to our own experiences as members of the middle class. As this phase of our thinking evolved, we did a second book, with an anthropologist, in which we tried to explore the implications for and the role of the middle class in the kinds of social change that occur when liberation theology and economics speak to each other. The outcome of this newer analysis was more specific, but the claims and the policy proposals still had much of the generic quality of "here's what the 'society' can do." We focused in that book on describing the condition of powerlessness, which we contend ties together the interests of all of us in the lower and middle fractions of the "working class," those whose economic destiny is controlled by others, not themselves. We did indeed personalize the issues, but we had not yet realized the extent to which our own personal experiences within Granville, Ohio, fit the analytic model we were developing. We knew that powerlessness invaded our own lives, but we did not articulate the examples that would make this knowledge come alive.

To a significant degree this current project came about because we began that articulation. The modern North American and global environmental movements that began in the 1960s, and have continued to grow ever since, were attempts to empower the middle class, and we pointed to them in our earlier work. As we probed the issues surrounding the environment and began to see how sustainability fit into the intellectual framework for social change that we had been building, our personal and professional lives slowly came together. Personally, we wanted very much to slow the pace of economic development in our own community because we were concerned about the sustainability of our local ecological system and our own quality of life. But those concerns brought us up against the very powerlessness that was at the center of our writing about social change. Our intellectual exploration of the appropriate connections between nature and human society led us to think about community in different ways. Alternative visions of community and some sense of a common good seem to be precisely what our own village needs as it wrestles with finding the appropriate balance between healthy change and the maintenance of a desirable quality of life.

We are not unique in becoming aware of the environment and its degradation. Any number of publications and events over the past three decades have captured the public's imagination and focused attention on the environment. Awareness that human activity, especially human economic activity, was poisoning the environment first became widespread after the publication of *Silent Spring* by Rachel Carson in 1961. Public concern was again raised by the first Earth Day in 1970. Awareness of the finite nature of our economic resources accompanied the publication of the Club of Rome's *Limits to Growth* in 1972, and E. F. Schumaker awakened us to the possibility of less-intrusive technology with *Small Is Beautiful* in 1973. In the mid-1970s, Love Canal taught us about the pervasiveness of the danger from buried chemical wastes. The ultimate thermodynamic limits to growth were popularized by Jeremy Rifkin's *Entropy* in 1980, and Jonathan Schell gave us a more philosophical view of our own indifference and even malice in *Fate of the Earth* in 1982. We worried about our global progress in the celebration of the twentieth anniversary of Earth Day in 1990 and the convening of the Earth Summit in 1992.

There is little doubt that we and the public have paid some attention, that the revelations from each of these sources have shocked us, and that in little ways we have "done something." Unfortunately, what we have not done is to generalize and internalize widespread human complicity in the issues. We typically react only when environmental degradation has a direct effect on our individual well-being. But we do not act, either instinctively or willfully, as a community when degradation affects other people, other generations, or other species. The recognition that the "fate of the earth" is our fate as well, that the piercing of the ozone layer pierces us too, does not even provoke self-interest, much less create a new, more communal consciousness.

Yet, environmental degradation is indisputable and insidious. Virtually everyone in the United States can talk about pollution in terms of smog in Los Angeles. But that easy identification does not help us to become aware of the interlocking causes that make environmental degradation so pervasive. In virtually every category where we might keep a "scorecard," the quality of the environment, its ability to sustain all kinds of life, is lower now than it was fifty years ago. Since the end of World War II, of all the land that is vegetated and/or used for agricultural purposes, some 17 percent, or about 1.9 billion hectares, has been seriously degraded by erosion or other problems that contaminate or eliminate topsoil.[2] Is it any wonder that global hunger is an escalating problem? It is interesting that even though the useable resource base continues to grow, projections show that it cannot keep up with population growth. For example, the worldwide fish catch is expected to grow by 20 percent between 1990 and 2010. But, because of population growth, that will still mean 10 percent less fish per person.[3] There are other indicators of the pernicious attacks on the integrity of the resource base that supports us all. These include the 0.4 percent annual rate of increase in carbon dioxide in the atmosphere, largely as a result of fossil-fuel burning and deforestation;[4] or the fact that during the twentieth century the amount of water used to support agriculture for human beings increased sixfold[5] while the world human population increased a little less than fourfold.[6]

Our illustration of the conditions in Granville and our global assessment highlight the problems, but they also disguise the fact that the burden of degradation is not evenly distributed. East Liverpool, Ohio, is not far from our small town, but it is an ecological victim, while most of our problems are self-inflicted. It is not by accident that East Liverpool became the site for a Waste Technology Industries incinerator. The town matched the profile of communities least likely to organize to protect their environmental and health interests. "The per capita income is less than $8,300. Sixty-two percent of the households make less than $19,000 per year. Only 6 percent of the population are college graduates, 37 percent are forty-five years of age or older, 18 percent are sixty-five or older. East Liverpool did not know it was a virtual advertisement for hazardous waste companies."[7] The known health effects from pollutants created by the incinerator include "cancer, birth defects, reproductive dysfunction, neurological damage."[8] In addition to the victimization of the community at large, East Liverpool is an exquisite example of environmental racism. Of the 13,000 population, 500 are African American. Not surprisingly, 100 percent of that group lives near the incinerator that converts waste products into energy. We will explore this issue further later in this chapter, but it seems clear that there is a consistent linkage between race, class, and the incidence of environmental degradation.

The consistent consequences of all this change, both globally and individually, are that the resources still available per person are shrinking and their quality is declining. And often, when human beings temporarily escape these consequences, they do so by transferring the impact to nature. Water resources provide an example of that. In the early part of this century, freshwater was abundantly available, most of it was clean, and it was largely free. Excessive use has led to a situation in which much of the freshwater has to be extensively treated before it is usable and the cost of acquiring and using water has risen dramatically. At least for a while, some humans can protect themselves from these consequences, but nature cannot consciously do that and as a result nonhuman species are damaged by this short-sighted anthropocentric behavior. Humans can buy bottled water; animals and trees cannot.

The Objectification of Nature in Economics

The response of human beings to any public disorder is usually to turn to the individual and reshape his or her mind-set. That has its importance, for the ecocrisis originates in us and will not be abetted unless we act to change things. But we need to recognize that the reality of sustaining the crisis is not centered in us but in the world we have externalized. Institutions and systems perpetuate what human beings at one time originated. These structures have a life of their own and continue to order behavior until we willfully withdraw our consent and establish new arrangements that serve different values. Economics is a dominant player in this process.

It is consequential to focus on the difference that might be created if environmental analysis within our disciplines moved in a direction that changed the prevailing view of nature from "something to be analyzed" to a "category of analysis." The first assumes that nature is important only because it is useful to us; the second that nature has value in its own right. There is a difference between investigating rain forests only because they do or might provide benefits to human beings and investigating them because they are intrinsically valuable. The former approach only looks at how our use of nature affects us; the latter examines how nature itself may be affected. Furthermore, the first approach implies that we may or may not "look at nature" in a particular situation; the second demands that every situation *must* be examined from the point of view of nature. There would be major ecological consequences to starting with the intrinsic value of nature rather than its instrumental value.

In the approach of most economists, it is assumed that the environment exists to serve human needs. They talk about "environmental amenities and disamenities" and treat the amenities as "resources" to be used in accomplishing specific, clearly economic goals, such as energy consumption and goods production. As we will argue later, economics is not unique in treating environmental issues in an anthropocentric way.

When one makes a move from the traditional economic treatment of the environment to one that focuses on its ecological base, there is more involved than just a name change. Traditional environmental economics implies the use of economic tools to achieve an "appropriate" mix of production, environmental amenity, and environmental damage.[9] "Appropriate" in this case means a mix that approximates the one that would result if all resources had prices affixed to them to reflect their "real" value in the eyes of all the economic actors currently on the scene.

If a large percentage of the population placed a high value on clean air, then there would be a high price attached to using the air as a dumping ground for waste products. While this might "solve" the problem of air pollution for the current generation, it does very little to represent the wishes of future generations. And it represents only the wishes of those human actors who have some way of expressing their valuation of clean air.

Ecological economics, on the other hand, attempts to lay the foundation for "sustainable" economic development. "Sustainable" implies that the level of economic activity is such that it allows for future economic and environmental services to be provided at a level at least as good as the current one.[10] This is still essentially anthropocentric, a "how should we use nature" approach, but at least it expands the notion of societal wellbeing by suggesting that our own use of the world's resources must be constrained so that future generations have just as much ability to draw on that resource base as we did. That is, they must have just as good a chance to enjoy the use of manufactured goods, eat healthy food, breathe clean air, or drink pure water as we did. Another way to express that idea is to say that even if current use of the air as a dumping ground for waste products were allocated exactly as current users of air wish it to be, if the prices were all appropriate, there would still not be appropriate use of the air if current use degraded the quality of the air in such a way that some future generation would have a reduced ability to use the air. To satisfy the sustainability requirement, that future generation must have access to air that is qualitatively just as good as the air available to the current generation.

As we have suggested, however, such an approach is still anthropocentric; the users it is concerned with, in any generation, are still human beings. And, it also begs the question as to which human beings are "most" important. Who suffers the consequences of today's reduced resource use? How are the future benefits distributed? There is a real danger here of creating a royal "we," one human and elitist.

While this human-centered concern for sustainability is preferable to current behavior, it addresses only our future in nature, not the future of nature itself. When we suggested viewing nature as a category of analysis, we meant viewing it as important in itself, something that has intrinsic value. Then any environmental or ecological analysis must be examined in terms of how it affects nature per se, not just how its impact on nature affects human beings.

Beginning with sustainability and with nature as a category of analysis changes the economic analysis of environmental issues. The conventional approach tends to look at any environmental question in a cost-benefit framework. In effect, it assumes that private-sector decision making will effectively deal with the internal private costs and benefits of a production or consumption decision. If I am making a decision about driving my own car to work, economic analysis assumes that I will carefully examine the benefits such as pleasure, saving of time, and convenience. I will weigh that against the costs imposed on me—such as stress, auto depreciation, and alternative uses of money—and will make a decision that maximizes my personal well-being. But that decision is not a purely private one because the decision to drive also imposes some costs on others in the form of increased traffic congestion and air pollution. Since these costs are external to the persons benefiting from the driving, they are called negative externalities or social costs because what increases my individual well-being may reduce someone else's.

In a world where the market worked well, the price of driving in the form of initial investment, operation, maintenance, and taxes would effectively reflect the interaction between private costs and benefits. It does not, however, provide any compensation for those who must bear the social cost of the decision to drive. Environmental policy based on conventional economic analysis is focused on changing the price paid to drive via gasoline taxes or emission control regulations in order to make that price adequately reflect those social costs. The damage done by the externalities would then be either reduced as the rising costs discouraged driving or compensated for by payments to those affected.

The conventional analysis assumes that if only we can find the appropriate price change and payment mechanisms, the problem will be solved. Imagine how this logical solution is affected and then affected once again as we move to "sustainable development" and then "nature as a category of analysis." Sustainability arguments would contend that the solution is inadequate if there is a negative externality or social cost that causes some damage that reduces the ability of others to use the biosphere, and those others are not represented in the bargaining process, which sets the price and compensation levels. Everyone who is currently damaged by the externalities associated with driving might be adequately compensated by reduced driving and/or payment. Sustainability, however, demands that future generations have as many resources at their command as the present generation. It is possible that long-lasting effects of the externality might have an impact on future generations. That is, the breathability of their air might be affected by current decisions to drive. And yet, they aren't here yet, so they cannot be adequately represented in the bargaining process.

Using nature as a category of analysis further compounds the problem. It is a truism to describe the biosphere as a large set of interactive and interdependent systems. That being the case, it is not possible to argue that individual actions will not affect the environment, the natural system. The goal of analysis, then, ought to be finding ways to act that affect the system of nature as little as possible. In this example, it means that even sustainability is not enough if sustainability focuses only on human ability to use the environment.

Perhaps a change in the example at this point will make the three cases clearer. There has been a long-standing controversy about Northwest lumbering and the spotted owl. Beginning in 1972, biologists in Oregon became aware of a conflict between the harvesting of old-growth timber and the preservation of the habitat for the northern spotted owl. Since the early twentieth century, the U.S. Forest Service and the Bureau of Land Management have had established practices with regard to multiple-use management of federal lands. The multiple uses include timber and mineral extraction and the management of populations of game species. Given that particular focus on human use of the forest, it makes sense to harvest the old-growth timber because as it decays, it is losing value as lumber while at the same time making a less than desirable habitat for game species.

The old-growth forest was seen (by the Forest Service) largely as a biological desert, providing a home for few significant animals, none of which were in much demand. In addition, the inaccessibility of these forests made them of limited use to forest recreationists.[11]

On the other hand, the old-growth timber provides extensive habitat for nongame animal species as well as plants. The northern spotted owl is a particular species whose nesting, and thus reproduction, takes place almost exclusively in the old-growth forest. At one level, the issue can be seen as "owls versus jobs," but from an ecological perspective that is just too simplistic. Many biologists saw the extensive plans for sale and harvesting of the old-growth forest as a threat to biological diversity in general. For them the owl, while important in itself, was also a symbol of the way in which ecosystems connect so that actions that seem on the surface to be relatively benign turn out to have consequences for the whole web of interrelated ecological communities. The extensive planned harvest of old-growth timber could decrease biodiversity in unexpected ways, and that would affect the health of the web and all its members.

With conventional analysis, the situation would be relatively simple— balance the private and social human benefits of extensive logging against the private and social human costs, including whatever value we place on the spotted owl. In economic parlance, we maximize the total social welfare by extending logging activity until the marginal benefits match the marginal costs. If that means losing the species, so be it.

Sustainability calls on us to ask that future generations be adequately represented in the bargaining. Thus, the logging can only be carried to the point where future generations will be just as able to draw lumber from the forests as is the current generation. And future generations must have the ability to enjoy the forest aesthetically, as well, and that may include an appreciation of the diversity of species. The spotted owl could still disappear, but only if we find some way to adequately represent both future and present generations in the bargaining process and then discover that all generations place a very low value on the survival of that species.

Thinking of nature as a category would almost certainly lead to the preservation of the spotted owl because the argument would begin with the assumption that the owl has rights too, that it is part of a complex ecological web of life, and that there is no a priori reason to assume the primacy of human rights at the expense of the web. Such a recognition of nature would elevate the importance of biodiversity in a healthy ecosystem; complexity creates both stability and survivability. That does not mean that we could not, in a particular case, evaluate a situation and decide that the survival of one species should take precedence over the survival of another. But this does not seem to be a situation that calls for that. There is no doubt that human economic hardship existed in the Northwest. Unfortunately, conventional economic analysis would countenance a solution to that hardship that has the side effect of destroying at least one other species. At the same time, many of the proponents of that analysis have consistently rejected the alternative of intra-human redistribution of income as a solution. With conventional analysis, the desire to protect the status quo may be as much of a problem as anthropocentrism.

Eventually, the problem of the spotted owl was "solved" by placing the owl on the endangered species list, an action that limited the ability of the Forest Service and others to damage owl habitat. While this solution has worked, it is not an optimal approach.

> The only way to have a proactive program for sensitive species management is to focus more completely on the ecosystem level. . . . Healthy ecosystems insure the protection of species-level diversity, while healthy

species may not insure the protection of other needed aspects of biological diversity. . . . We can probably grow owls through captive propagation and inter-habitat transfers of genetic stock if that is the primary concern, but in doing so, much of the ultimate objective in having an endangered species law is lost.[12]

As our examples illustrate, environmental degradation is a reality; it is extensive, pervasive, and growing. And its effects are felt more and more by those least able to resist, the poor and minorities in our human communities, and the endangered species in our natural communities. We have argued that it rests, at least in part, on an excessively individualistic and anthropocentric vision of the world, a vision that is reinforced by economic analyses that fail to recognize the importance of intergenerational interactions and holistic ecological communities. And we will also argue that it is further reinforced by theologies that are indifferent to nature. Overcoming those problems will require new values and new analyses.

The Silence of Liberation Theology

One of the obvious reasons why our previous work ignored the environment and ecological relationships was that the liberation theology we wanted to contextualize in the middle class has focused on human social oppression. The cry of pain in the Third World, and among women and blacks, has been shaped most immediately by history and by the social, economic, and political conditions of the global order. To say that theology is done "after the sun goes down" means reflection occurs after a day of struggling for social justice in the human sphere. To be sure, some of that oppression has involved and even been exacerbated by exploitation of the environment. But until recently liberation theology has not concerned itself with the issues of ecological survival that arise when the sun is up and the ozone has been depleted. A theology preoccupied with the events of the Exodus and the event of Jesus appears to fit the circumstances of the historical-social sphere more readily than those of the biosphere. Hence, the question for those of us who are persuaded by liberation theology is: Can a theology that is primarily focused on social transformation by infusing the historical order with a liberative God address ecological disaster with the same force? Can the God who is centered in the struggle for liberation also be seen centered as clearly in nature's struggle for ecological survival? Can God be understood as a "spiritual power within all of creation"?[13]

When we turn our attention to the sphere of nature, we confront a curious irony. On the one hand, environmentalism has been a middle-class project in recent decades. On the other hand, some who have been marginalized have argued that gravitation toward ecological issues is an escape from facing the questions of historical oppression. But that is a futile distraction if in fact the middle class is as powerless as we have argued! There is something bordering on the absurd when many in our own small community commit themselves to recycling while twenty-four hours a day a factory in the next town billows flakes of fiberglass into the air and our schools and churches are already contaminated by asbestos. We may do our share as individuals in small and committed ways, but it is precisely as individuals that we are powerless before the real environmentally consequential forces. It would seem realistic to assume that liberation theology, the middle class, and the prevailing economic order are all ill-suited for this ecological task. Separately and together they often draw their momentum from anthropocentric interests.

What are the terms on which theology might become functional in relation to environmental issues? In the mid-1950s theologian John Bennett and Hebrew Scriptures scholar James Muilenburg were debating the place of nature before a fascinated and partisan group of students. Muilenburg pointed out triumphantly that the term for nature did not even appear in Scripture. Bennett responded that the word may not be there but there is an awful lot of it! Nature is indeed prominent but it is not clear that its relationship to history is always established convincingly. One wonders why Muilenberg did not say what Rosemary Radford Ruether wrote in a later time: "The Hebraic understanding of the God of Israel did not set history against nature, but rather experienced God as Lord of heaven and earth, whose power filled all aspects of their lives."[14] Whatever the biblical tradition may or may not contribute to the debate, our theological legacy of the last few centuries has done too little to clarify the issue. That in large measure is because the discussion of nature within theology has been diminished by the increased credibility of the natural sciences. When Friedrich Schleiermacher wanted to explain the form of God's earthly management, it was equated with the laws of nature as described by the natural scientist; that is, nature's laws are God's laws. Fearing the fusion of a God who acts in history with natural processes, Karl Barth withdrew the orbit of nature from any revelational traces; history alone, and not nature, is where the primary acts of God are evident. While there are significant middle-ground positions, our heritage is more often marked by either alienation from religion or assimilation into a scientific agenda. It would appear more promising to some to look outside our contaminated biblical and theological traditions for an operational model.

Liberation theologians *are* beginning to approach the issue of the environment. Among some the tendency has been to add the environment to the existing list of economic, political, and social issues. Each can quite properly be examined as a sphere of domination. It has been suggested that the environment only needs to be drawn in as one more category within which exploitation occurs. Political theology does this as well; Jürgen Moltmann talked about "the vicious circles of death."[15] He discussed four spheres of oppression, of which the "industrial pollution of nature" was one. Moltmann asserted that the vicious circles are "bound up with each other" but did not articulate how.

We need a way of approaching the issue of natural and historical processes that features them as interlocking and interpenetrating spheres. Adding one more sphere does not quite get us there. One of the strengths of liberation theology is that it has taught us to begin in the location in which we find ourselves, particularly as observed by the social sciences, rather than in scripture and tradition. What some might seek in theory liberation theologians find given in the concrete reality of the natural order. The following illustration tries to show what this means in the context of a real-world experience; it illumines the interlocking and interpenetrating dimensions that tie together the economic, social, and political realities.

One of the most fundamental needs of our society is electricity. In the United States it is certainly a condition for even a minimal standard of living. It has joined air and water as one of the necessary elements in our daily living. But the combination sets an interesting environmental problem, which upon analysis reveals how the political, economic, social, and environmental spheres interlock and interpenetrate.

Smokestacks may not be as visible in some communities as in others, but we all tend to identify them with pollution. Electricity is most often produced by burning fossil fuels. The consequence is that sulfur and nitrous oxides—waste products—go into the air and when combined with water vapor create acid rain. That rain is thought to be the principal culprit in damaging and killing forests and lakes in the northeastern United States. We may not fully understand that but we recognize it is not good. Now we are in a position to see an economic problem as well as to explore how to reduce the pollution. What economists call an "externality" has come into play in that a cost is emerging in the Northeast that is not being paid for by the producers and users of electricity in the Midwest. The most obvious move is to install scrubbers in the smokestacks. That reduces the oxides flowing into the atmosphere, presumably at a cost to the producer but eventually to the consumer. But the scrubber uses water to clean the air, and the oxides combined with water now exist as sludge, which needs to be disposed of. The problem has not really gone away; there is still an externality; it has just taken a different form, and the cost is still real to someone.

The political dimension of producing electricity comes into play in determining whether the acid rain or the sludge is the worst form of pollution generated by the production process. We can endure higher costs for electricity or endure the costs of acid rain. Either move is going to result in some unemployment. If rising costs of electricity prevail in midwestern states, those more industrialized areas with higher usage will experience unemployment. If the acid rain is created in the Midwest so as to keep costs down and employment up, northeastern states will take the hit in terms of damage to forests that are crucial for the lumbering industry and lakes that are essential for the tourist industry. The political form of the issue, then, is in terms of who has the power to divert unemployment from their sector to some other.

At this point a social dimension comes into view. The issue before us can, in some way, be solved economically and politically. But, in the process, some group in the society is going to get hurt and of course some group is going to benefit. That thrusts us into a consideration of class, something most Americans pretend does not exist. And, of course, in our society class issues continue to be inextricably bound up with issues of race and gender. Different social groups are involved in absorbing the consequences of one decision or another. The consequences in the Northeast will largely be borne by rural constituencies, generally lower-middle-class persons. In the Midwest two groups are involved: an owner/managerial group that controls the means of production, and organized labor, which is again part of the working, wage-earning class. One thing is clear no matter what decision is made: some group at or near the bottom will bear the brunt of the unemployment.

What is helpful about the illustration is that it moves us beyond the notion of levels, circles, or categories that line up either vertically or horizontally but do not interpenetrate or interlock. It shows us how in the situation of pollution the spheres are integrally related. In this example, the environment is not an "add-on," but is central to the spheres of economic tension and oppression within which the theology of liberation is at ease. Rather than being driven by the need to invent some integrating scheme, we find that the situation itself generates one.

One of the things that make liberation theology compatible with this illustration is that domination is a common theme. In our discussion of the East Liverpool example, we briefly mentioned the excessive impact of the incinerator pollution on the African American community. In the United States, the African American community is often victimized by the union of racism and environmental injustice. Emilie M. Townes notes, "Contemporary versions of lynching a whole people are toxic waste landfills in African-American communities. Toxic waste facilities are often located in southern communities that have high percentages of the poor, the elderly, the young and people of color. . . . Southern Black rural communities are home to large commercial hazardous waste landfills, disposal facilities, and incinerators."[16] Often these communities are seduced by promises of a positive economic trade-off in jobs and standards of living. This "environmental extortion"[17] seldom translates into real economic advantage and always incurs a severe health deficit, which itself becomes a negative economic consequence.

Environmental racism suggests that our institutions are set up in such a way that the negative environmental externalities associated with any action are always visited most heavily on racial and ethnic minorities as well as others who are economically and politically powerless. "*Environmental racism* refers to any policy, practice, or directive that differentially affects or disadvantages (whether intended or unintended) individuals, groups, or communities based on race or color. . . . [It] combines with public policies and industry practices to provide *benefits* for whites while shifting industry *costs* to people of color."[18] It is easy to understand how this can happen, both in terms of pollution creation and pollution treatment. The "not in my backyard" philosophy that so many practice means that pollution-generating businesses are always going to be pushed to the least desirable locations, those with the lowest land values. But given the inequality in the distribution of income between white males and all others in our society, those locations are also the places most likely to be housing sites for people of color and the poor in general. And if the operation of any kind of treatment facility is likely to have negative side effects, its location will also be shifted to the neighborhood of those with low amounts of economic and political power. Responses like that make it easy for those in power to believe something is being done about pollution when in reality nothing is being changed.

Such domination cannot be the only integrating theme in approaching the political, economic, social, and environmental spheres because it does not fully illustrate the interlocking and interpenetrating feature that is articulated in the electricity illustration. Yet it *is* what each of the spheres has in common. It hardly needs to be argued that environmental crises are a result of exploitation of the natural order. And domination is set up in the economic alternatives, the political determination of whose interests will prevail, and the class and race dimensions of who bears the consequences. Any resolution is finally a "question of power: who wields it and what sort it is."[19] And that has consequences for the status of nature.

The Triangle of Science, Economics, and Theology

The value premises that have been dominant in the United States during the last fifteen years or so have led to a public policy emphasis aimed at increased voluntary efforts, usually by individuals, to address public problems; we are challenged to reduce the public problem of pollution by encouraging individuals to behave differently. That, however, does not address problems at the level of institutional power, which creates and perpetuates poverty, powerlessness, or pollution. Without changing the system, individuals of good heart find themselves confronted by intractable structures where all of the power is in the hands of those who benefit from the status quo. If we want to stop pollution and empower nature, we have to create a system that makes it more and more costly to maintain that entrenched power. In the rest of this chapter, we will identify some of the structural causes for the degradation of the ecosystem.

One of the most obvious points one could make is that nature itself did not spawn our ecocrisis. Its apocalyptic proportions, most would agree, have their origins in the human species. But it is not enough to simply go to the human heart and find it wanting, driven by greed toward privileges and unwilling to accept responsibility. In addition, the systems of thought we use to analyze life and nature shape the conditions under which the earth suffers. We suggest there is an unholy and unrecognized alliance between some of the analyses in our own disciplines of economics and theology and those within science. On their own and in their interaction these analyses exacerbate the deterioration of the biosphere. Some may assume that the disciplines themselves are benign and therefore not culpable; in fact they profoundly influence our viewing—what we choose to look at and how we see it. One does not need to be reading a textbook in economics to be under the spell of its assumptions. As John Maynard Keynes argued so forcefully sixty years ago, "Madmen in authority, who hear voices in the air, are distilling their frenzy from some academic scribbler of a few years back."[20] In reality, analyses arising in economics, theology, and science, among others, have often programmed a relationship to the natural order that violates its interests and advances the crisis. And they have had an impact on each other. No discipline operates independently of others. In this case, science has been a formative player in the ways in which both economics and theology have defined themselves.

It is not our intention to engage in science bashing. The scientific disciplines are not alone in their tendency to be "directed toward the domination of objects and facts."[21] Indeed, there is another side—many in modern science have engaged in self-correction, with an attempt to be more holistic and consider both the relations and setting of particular phenomena; Rachel Carson was, after all, a scientist. Yet one cannot overlook the dimension of science that strives for power and domination, the discovery and generation of laws to "explain" and hence control nature. Some will say that this really is technology rather than science. Yet one cannot escape the sense that "knowledge is power." The determination to discover "nature's laws" is hardly benign; it is a precondition for domination. At some level science cannot be free of the goal of making nature work for us. It could be argued that no one has more respect for nature than the scientist. But respect does not necessarily award intrinsic value. Both science and its application in the development of new technology are disposed to approach nature as an object over which the human subject seeks control. That approach is not likely to be very active in resurrecting nature or placing the "rights" of nature on an equal footing with the "rights" of humans.

And, of course, anthropocentrism is certainly not confined to science. It is a part of and flows into all modes of inquiry. Economic analysis and the resulting economic systems, as interpreted both by the left and the right, are preoccupied with allocating scarce resources in such a way as to maximize material *human* welfare. Faced with perceived injustice to humans, economists almost always respond with proposals to foster growth in the output of material goods and services. Whatever basic principles are espoused or institutions established, the essential premise is always that *humans*, or at least some of them, will be better served and that, as a result, society's welfare will be enhanced. But there is nothing in the typical canons of economic analysis that attaches intrinsic value to nature. Indeed, the commitment to growth has been a prime source for the objectification and resulting degradation of nature; society has over-valued material gain and undervalued the impact of the degradation. Both conventional and radical economics show themselves to be consistently anthropocentric; the goal is "goods and services" *for human beings.* Attention to nature as object can of course occur, especially as it may become clear that it is not productive to ignore the natural order. But any claims for nature as subject, as having standing in its own right, as something more than setting and resource, must finally come from outside economics. Until recently, economics has been wedded to the *use* of the natural order for human purposes, and limits on that use have been largely erected in terms of resource depletion, which is important only because it constrains the possibilities for further growth in human consumption. When the abuse of nature impacts the creation of wealth and its distribution, it gets the attention of economists, but the intrinsic value of nature is certainly not established thereby.

Of all the disciplines, theology deserves the most severe criticism. That is not because it has more influence, or even at times as much, but because in its heritage it has the resources for an appropriate valuation of nature. Even though its ecological promise is compromised by the apparent priority of human history as the arena for God's acts,[22] it also has access to themes that might reflect the intrinsic value of nature. The biblical record provides some conspicuous examples, with its honoring of land and its use of nature as an example to articulate understanding of God's work. However, much of theology has also succumbed to anthropocentrism and yielded to a patriarchal disposition in ways that contribute directly to the crisis. It may be true that "a seizure of power over nature is not intended,"[23] but the notion of "subduing the earth" has contributed to a dramatic presumption in favor of the human species and its interests. The slide from dominion to domination is difficult to arrest. Nearly thirty years have passed since Lynn White Jr. grounded the ecological crisis in the Hebrew/Christian tradition. He argued that the creation stories appear to authorize a view of nature as something we are free to have "dominion over." The argument of this church historian has been challenged and at some level refuted but our culpability has not been finally exorcised. To some degree traditional interpretations of the Judeo-Christian story have authorized a view of nature that perceives it as the "theater" for the real drama of God and God's people. Nature is the stage but human history is the arena of revelation and response. In more recent times mainstream theology has compounded its complicity in the degradation of nature by retreating from it before the advance of science. To cover their own vulnerability in the modern era, where science appears to explain the origins and the dynamics of the earth, some theologians have muted the relationship of God to nature while elevating history, and, as a consequence, deprived the dialogue over nature of theological resources.

In the United States, at least, and probably in much of the industrial world, we have adopted these dominant perspectives of science, economics, and theology; thus, the mainstream analyses of our intellectual lives have contributed to the subversion of nature and supported its conversion into an object "for" the human subject. As citizens we may not always intuitively recognize how those analyses seep into our consciousness or sense of reality. But they are part of how we think and react. Through our culture we inherit assumptions about nature that are rooted in disciplines and theories we may never have studied. For example, one does not need to read theology or even be self-consciously religious to be a mediator or bearer of its values. The same is true for the values inherent in science and economics. Even without our conscious adherence to them those values have supported the creation of strong sets of institutions and structural arrangements that assure that we make decisions and do business in ways that deprive nature of any intrinsic noninstrumental value.

We recognize the important role that science has played in the creation of this problem and can play in its reversal. But as a theologian and an economist, we are especially interested in exploring and exposing the ways in which the analyses of our particular disciplines have contributed to the degradation of nature. Since the dominant analyses subvert nature, society needs new alternative theological and economic analyses that move nature to the center, analyses that recognize that human beings are, in fact, a part of nature, not a dominant force appointed to control it.

Individualism and Human Dignity

Attempts to redress environmental problems are often intercepted by our commitment to individualism. By individualism we mean the disposition to think in terms of our own interests and to act, or not, without external restraint. As the issues of the environmental impact of development have arisen in our community, some have argued, "It is an individual's land, and he or she should be able to use it in whatever way he or she sees fit." Those who have become alarmed, enraged, and horrified about potential damage to the community become actively engaged only when the damage hits home in their own lives and neighborhoods. Perhaps that is because pollution and its effects are most often seen as public problems, while our strident and often fierce individualism focuses singularly on the private self: self-improvement is our task, self-reliance is our destiny, and self-interest is the means toward our fulfillment. Each of us is finally answerable only to ourselves. Personal choice drives our ethic and freedom means being left alone by others, especially government. From this perspective, the community is no more than a collection of individuals; they shape the community, but it does not shape them. The collective ethos concerns itself only with the protection of singularity; justice finally entails only the preservation of *my* rights; there is really no such thing as the *common* good.

Unfortunately, as we shall see, environmental degradation often arises from the collective excesses of individualistic behavior, especially in the economic sphere. And it is a problem that seems so vast that we may view ourselves as powerless to implement change. On the one hand, our dominant economic and political values are mostly entwined with the behavior of individual human beings, while on the other hand the problems we face seem to have both causes and solutions that are communal. And even when we have communal impulses there are precious few communal structures to support them. Is it any wonder that we often feel overwhelmed in the face of institutional arrangements that seem destructive of our interests and out of our control?

Addressing these issues calls for both new values and new institutions to implement them. One possibility we must face is that we have become blind to the reality that human nature only gets fully defined within the context of social groups or communities. Our commitment to individualism may have shaped the structures of economic relationships like class, division of labor, and patterns of ownership in such a way that we believe all such relationships to be individual. But it is the mutual interaction within a community that provides us with our only opportunity to become fully human. We have allowed our values to be shaped by the narrow perceptions of utilitarian thought, which directs us to view our connections with others as only instrumental. And that is especially true of our economic activity. As we have suggested, the dominant language of modern economics focuses on nature, and even human beings, as simply "resources" to be used in the pursuit of individual material well-being. Thus, as long as individualism dominates our value system it will be impossible for us to change significantly the economic system and its supporting institutions.

The ultimate expression of our individualism and the heart of our environmental problem lie in our excessively anthropocentric view of the natural world. As long as we accord nature no intrinsic value, viewing it as only instrumental, then it will remain easy to use and abuse the natural world in the service of the needs of individual human beings. Since our dominant individualism allows us to treat even other human beings as only instrumental, it is little wonder that we also continue to mistreat nature and, in the process, foul our own nest.

Some have argued that significant change will occur if we set human dignity rather than the individual at the center of our economic mission. In his 1995 presidential address to the Association for Social Economics, Mark Lutz[24] talked about the centrality of human dignity to the mission of economics. The universality of human dignity as a value implies that economic institutions, whatever form they might take, must accord more than mere instrumentality to their participating human actors. These actors must have agency, an active role in controlling and directing those institutions. And since human dignity is a right that crosses over generational boundaries, all human actors, past, present, and future, possess that dignity in equal measure and thus have equal rights to the level of economic well-being necessary to implement human dignity. The locus for the implementation of dignity and for the extension of economic well-being is the community, not the individual.[25] That is because human dignity is mutually shared by all. These arguments help to push us a long way toward justifying new kinds of economic institutions that eschew overpowering individualism in favor of structures that are communal, humanizing, and empowering.

One corollary of this thesis is that ecological sustainability is a right that flows from the universality of human dignity;[26] future human beings have the same degree of dignity as present ones, and therefore should have the same right to draw upon the resources of the ecosystem. Since we, too, are concerned about issues of environmental degradation, we want to carry that argument a step further. Lutz's argument is consistent with the enlightenment/human reason ideas that underlie orthodox economic analysis. He contends that it is our very human agency and its associated dignity that set us apart from nature, make us superior to it. That is, human beings have agency but nature is only instrumental. In his analysis, dignity is an attribute that flows from the fact of agency. Lutz is right: only human beings have agency in his sense; we act purposively for ends we consider to be worthwhile.[27] It would be nice to believe that the responsible exercise of human agency across generations would lead to ecological sustainability. We are afraid, however, that the elevation of this value has helped to set up a dominant/subordinate relationship with nature, which ultimately leads to our destruction of nature. The misuse of agency may permit us and indeed lead us to abuse nature. But that flaw could be mended if the right of universal dignity were extended to reflect not just human dignity, but also the dignity of nature, the rights of other species. One of the arguments is that human beings have intrinsic value as part of creation; but if that is true then the other parts of creation should be intrinsically valuable as well.

The good side of the human dignity argument is that the sense of communal responsibility that flows from a mutual sense of dignity ought to authorize the best possible form of stewardship of the earth and its resources. The downside is that everything that is not human is viewed in just that way, as a resource, useable in whatever way is needed to serve human dignity. That is too anthropocentric a view to assure us of protection from the trap of environmental degradation.

The commitment to universal human dignity must, by definition, carry with it an end to interpersonal oppression and domination. Racism, classism, sexism cannot survive in the face of human dignity; one cannot respect the mutual dignity of all human beings and oppress some of them at the same time. In an analogous way, if we recognized the dignity of nature we would not be able to simultaneously degrade and destroy parts of it.

Individualism, however, is not the only source of environmental degradation; and most arguments are not fashioned around human dignity. Looking back only as far as 1970, we can document some other sources of the problems we face: human population growth that averaged about 1.8 percent per year; growth in the production (at 3.3 percent) and consumption (at 3.1 percent) of goods and services; the associated growth in the use of energy, particularly fossil fuels (at 2.7 percent); and the expansion of technology, which has created whole new categories of waste products to be absorbed by the biosphere. Added to this is the increasing disparity between rich and poor nations; there was an average difference of about $23,000 in per capita GNP between the forty-nine poorest countries and the twenty-four richest ones in 1994;[28] that has encouraged an even more frantic drive to create more material goods and services.

Two dominant economic values are reflected in these patterns of behavior: the first is that "societal welfare, the common good, should be measured in terms of material well-being," and the second is that "more is better." Those in turn are supported by the widespread belief in the economic paradigm that insists that scarcity is only a relative phenomenon, manageable via the judicious use of resource substitution. Continuous economic growth is no problem as long as we believe that technology and innovation will always produce adequate substitutes for any part of the environment that gets damaged or depleted in the process. Degradation is only a temporary phenomenon that may affect nature, but not human well-being. Furthermore, the long tradition of creation as a divine plan for *humanity* sustains our indifference to the natural order. Apparently even the eye of the divine is singularly focused on humankind and its salvation.

The elevation of the dignity of human beings and nature in order to mount an effective attack upon our environmental problems requires at least three changes in the status quo. First, we must recognize that while more for me may be better for me, it is not always better for society; we must strive not for continued material growth, but for a stable ecological system that can be sustained in the long run. Second, in order to achieve that we need to develop some new economic models, built on the reality of the absolute scarcity of at least some irreplaceable environmental resources. Third, all of these changes have to rest on a new set of values that displaces our human-centered view of the world. These three changes form a template for what we plan to accomplish in this book. As an economist and a theologian, we are committed to exploring ways in which we might use our analyses to help create an ecologically sensitive society that authorizes structures which reinforce the reality that humans are a part of nature.

We have some experience in thinking and writing about social change. As we pointed out in the introduction to this chapter, the two of us, together with an anthropologist, spent a few years contextualizing liberation theology within the middle class. The outcome was our book, *Risking Liberation: Middle Class Powerlessness and Social Heroism.* We argued that large portions of the "middle" class are, in reality, part of a sector more appropriately described as "laboring" class; we all earn wages or salaries rather than benefiting from owning productive resources. While we do not describe ourselves as oppressed, our control over the conditions or terms of our lives is marginal. We may not be victims but increasingly we are victimized. Anyone who has spent $20,000 on a new car that is certifiably a lemon and can't get satisfaction from the maker has at least a superficial understanding of powerlessness. We argued that the situation calls for us to overcome the individualism that is virulently present in our society and to develop a new sense of mutuality and solidarity on class terms. As a class we need to respond collectively, working for change together by reclaiming control over our destiny. That was the "social heroism" Weber argued had been missing since the Reformation. The lack of a sense of social identity is even more prominent in relation to nature and its degradation. That degradation is also systemic, and it too calls for solutions that reclaim the community's control over its own life.

Despite our critique of individualism, we cannot exempt the individual from responsibility. What is needed is a new consciousness in individuals *and* in the community that recognizes that they are nature rather than that they live off of nature. Nature is not other. A writer like Alice Walker speaks to us with a clear sense of a spiritual relationship with the earth. She not only has a deep sense of a God of freedom within creation but of her own existence as centered in the natural order. God cohabits both history and nature. In her work she develops a profound sense of kinship between some of her characters and otherkind. Walker herself communes with nature as intensely as a mother with her child. She writes of a day she "walked out into the countryside to listen to what the Earth was saying." For several hours "I was in intense dialogue with the trees."[29] We could probably think of that as nothing more than appreciation of nature until we hear the voice of Walker speaking through one of her characters. In *The Color Purple* Shug exclaims, "I knew that if I cut the tree, my arm would bleed."[30] Alice Walker's identification with nature leads her to solidarity as a committed environmentalist. Most of us do not make that commitment; we don't even recognize ourselves as part of nature. In the United States and other industrial countries we seem to be able to have an enthusiastic appreciation of nature unencumbered by any sense of identification or solidarity with it. We may be awestruck in the presence of its wonders, healed and restored by its beauty, even inspired by it to religious reflection, and yet we still think of ourselves as separate from and superior to nature. It is not us. We live in a steady state of "earth-denial and earth-disconnectedness," which at its deepest level translates into "earth-hating practices."[31]

T · W · O

Individualism and Community in Economics and Theology

Distancing ourselves from nature may not always be conscious or conspiratorial, but it is this "othering" that makes exploitation seem legitimate and inevitable. Autonomous individuals perceive themselves as subject and everything else as object. The consequences of individualism for the environment define the need for a revolution of inclusiveness. While many of us may never get to the point where we would *feel* with Shug, "I knew that if I cut the tree, my arm would bleed," we still need to *think* in a different mode. As Sallie McFague argues, what is called for is a sensibility "which is holistic and responsible, inclusive of all life forms, and that acknowledges the interdependence of all life."[1] The task of this chapter, and of this book as well, is to advocate community as a counterpoint to individualism; and it is a community in which "the interdependence of all life forms" is the integrating center.

Thinking about an inclusive community means, among other things, that thought patterns that are dualistic (e.g., mind/body, human/nature) and hierarchical (e.g., God-human-nature) must be consciously purged. Seeing all things as separates in competition with each other, and ranking everything, contributes to our thinking of nature and the environment as objects that are only there for us to use. Inclusiveness requires that our disciplines, in consort with each other, represent reality as relational, and we must understand particular entities in their connectedness. Recognizing that nature is a social construction, that it is what we see it to be, calls for a reconstruction of what and how we know. We act on the world as we see it, and if we see it as an object we will try to dominate and exploit it. Unlike other animals, "we have a *choice* in [shaping] the world we inhabit,"[2] and the choices we have made and do make are reflected in the analyses of our disciplines.

Clearly, our society and our disciplines have generally chosen options different from those we are advocating; and it was suggested in the previous chapter how those options gained credibility through some versions of science, economics, and theology. Nature has almost always been "other," and as other it is there for our conquest and use. Developers in our small village, national corporations, and their compatriots in government believe they have a right to redefine our landscape with fast food restaurants, efficient gas stations and motels, convenience marts, and waste-burning incinerators. They argue that owning the land legitimates using the land as they see fit. Their twist on things subverts "the best interest of the land" into "the most profitable use of it."

Once again Alice Walker has exposed that construction of nature: "Some of us have become used to thinking that woman is the nigger of the world, that a person of color is the nigger of the world, that a poor person is the nigger of the world. But, in truth, Earth itself has become the nigger of the world."[3] The depletion of the rain forests and the ozone layer, the threat of global warming, the decline in quality of drinking water and air, and the disappearance of a large number of species of animal and plant life during the last twenty years are but a few evidences that she is right. Our disposition to ignore these problems and exempt ourselves from responsibility can mask the severity of the "ecocide." But once again Walker dispels our illusions: "We are judged by our worst collective behavior, since it is so vast; not by our singular best. The Earth holds us responsible for our crimes against it, not as individuals, but as a species. . . . I found it to be a terrifying thought. For I had assumed that the Earth, the spirit of the Earth, noticed exceptions—those who wantonly damage it and those who do not. But the Earth is wise. It has given itself into the keeping of all, and all are therefore accountable."[4] Even enlightened individualism will not save us.

In our own recent work, we too have failed to be accountable to nature. We have focused on the issues of oppression and powerlessness, drawing on liberation theology, economic theory, and economic and political reality to address the systemic and structural obstacles to widespread empowerment of the marginalized. As we mentioned in the last chapter, in *Risking Liberation* we focused on the powerlessness of the middle class. Our perceived task was to articulate a pervasive experience of which we all are at least dimly aware. The goal was to awaken a sense of our social reality and the commonality of some of our experience and explore their distortion in the institutions of U.S. society. We identified liberation theology as one ideology that could play a role in enabling a "social heroism" and an associated drive for change to come into being. While liberation theology has oppression as its matrix—and the middle class is hardly oppressed—we have argued that the reality of powerlessness and its institutionalization can in fact relate to the themes of a liberation theology; oppression and powerlessness are at least cousins. But our work has been conspicuous in its failure to include ecological/environmental issues, to identify nature as powerless and oppressed, when we attempted to locate liberation theology within the economic, political, and social settings of the United States and the world. We did not see that the interlocking nature of oppression involves race, class, gender, *and* the earth. When we intercept "the power of nature to live its own life,"[5] we are in an arena where the human price is paid most fully by the poor, persons of color, and women. Now we want to redress that omission by asking the question: Can the same theology lead to "ecological heroism"? Can we recenter our disciplines in an inclusive community and exorcise the propensities toward individualism and anthropocentrism?

Community and the Economic Order

If we embrace a determination to think relationally and foreclose on "othering," one of the first issues that come to the table is the form of our economic order. What kind of system would arise from and contribute to the promotion of an inclusive community in which justice is a defining factor?

In the first chapter, we outlined an ecological approach to the issues of resource scarcity and resource use. The thrust of that analysis does push us toward more communal political and economic structures. That is an unusual move in today's world, where the bulk of the evidence would seem to support the position that social decision making is a bankrupt ideology. The dramatic changes in Eastern Europe certainly lend credence to an argument that market approaches to economic questions are more fruitful than centrally planned approaches. And, at the same time, more individualistic and democratic political structures are replacing centralized and authoritarian ones in Eastern Europe.

Nonetheless, we contend that the ethical and the economic imperatives contained in demands for sustainable development and the use of nature as a category of analysis do move us in the direction of communal rather than individual decision making. Justice is certainly not assured by more public decision making, but it seems more likely to emerge there than where power accumulates in the hands of small numbers of private individuals. We have argued that the economic dimensions of environmental problems stem from the divergence between social and private cost. Because attempts to develop private and individualistic solutions largely ignore social cost, they are doomed to failure.

To some extent, of course, the call for more socially responsible approaches to the ecosphere echoes from every direction and political venue. Almost everyone wants the damage to be reduced, and recognizes that it is a social need. In that sense, there is a widespread belief in some sort of social, communal response. Some, however, believe that the best way to accomplish that communal response, to achieve the common good, is by appealing to atomistic self-interest in a largely unregulated market economy. At the opposite end of the spectrum we find those who would allocate all scarce resources by means of some central plan that would recognize and account for absolute scarcity.

In the face of that range of views, our own approach clearly seeks a middle ground. We are convinced that individuals will not act effectively unless they see that a new approach to the environment serves *both* their own interests and those of the society. We take it as a given that we cannot totally abandon the market-oriented individualistic approach. However, we are also convinced that even the best-intentioned individuals cannot eliminate all of the divergence between social and private cost solely within the context of a private market system. Thus, some form of communal approach is inescapable. The issue is whether or not individual interests can be interpreted and constrained to serve the interests of the community. The difficulty in finding effective alternatives is exacerbated, as we have argued earlier, when we introduce the claims of future generations and nature itself.

There is a way to think through this dilemma without getting trapped in the tired, and probably outmoded, dogma of traditional socialism. That traditional rhetoric and its associated structures have failed in the sense that societies built on them do not seem to be able to survive economically or politically in the last decade of the twentieth century. Widespread demands for political and economic freedom have toppled virtually all of the old-line communist societies and seriously threatened the survival of the few that remain. We contend, however, that current political and economic fervor does not indicate a rejection of all the values that underlie this notion of community, but rather a rejection of the corrupt and authoritarian structures that grew up within modern communist/socialist societies.

At the most basic level, perhaps we can go back to slogans to think about the differences between capitalism and socialism, and then use those to show why some sort of socially responsive communal approach to resource allocation is necessary for sustainability. Capitalism suggests something like "from each according to ability, to each according to productivity," while socialism argues "from each according to ability, to each according to need." The difficulty on the distribution side of these sound bites is that it is perhaps impossible to gauge the productivity of future generations and of most nonhuman species. Indeed, if many claims about current economic injustice are true, we cannot even adequately measure the productive contributions of contemporary human beings, let alone the natural environment and the unborn. Therefore, if we use a strictly capitalist productivity-based approach to building an economic system, we will be too focused on the present, and that cannot create sustainability. We can, however, make some judgments about need that would allow us to identify what it means to have sustainability and to recognize nature as a category of analysis. At the most fundamental level, then, the distribution mechanism in our emerging economic system must be based on need, and therefore the system must be built on communal rather than individual values.

To put the argument in another way, capitalist market economies cannot respond to need with assurance, since market economies use the price system to respond to effective demand; those who can pay determine production, not those in need. A socialist system uses some sort of collective or communal social agency to evaluate and respond to "need," often without regard to ability to pay. We contend that the observed "failure" of socialism recently has much more to do with inappropriate decisions by social agencies than it does with the rejection of need-based distribution systems. Bureaucracies have a powerful tendency to continue with "traditional" solutions long after they have outlived their usefulness. And it does not seem to make much difference whether the bureaucracy is the planning agency in China, the Defense Department in the United States, or the management of IBM.

When the issue is one of poverty, we want to have an economic system that responds to need and gives priority to the cry of the hurting. What we get in most societies is an economic system that is tuned to respond to power. Power may be gained by means of accumulated wealth and income, or it may be gained by political control. Whichever the case, power typically serves the needs of the powerful, not the poor and the hurting. It is no different when we turn to the issue of environmental degradation. The dominant approaches to production and consumption, the primary sources of degradation, will again serve the needs of the powerful, not the needs of racial and ethnic minorities, future generations, or nonhuman species.

While both capitalism and socialism in their existing forms tend to ignore the environment, socialism at least has the decision-making structure that would allow it to pay attention. That is, when the goal for the allocation of resources is set by some social or communal agency, there is at least the possibility for paying attention to something beyond narrowly defined economic self-interest. On the other hand, with capitalism, all of the goals are in fact set by the "individual" owners of resources and the means of production.

It would be useful to develop the distinction between capitalism as a socio/politico/economic system and the market as a tool for allocating resources. A similar distinction can be made between socialism and central planning. Capitalism exists whenever the means of production are owned by private individuals or organizations and those individuals and organizations are reasonably free to use the means of production for their own purposes. Freely fluctuating prices then determine who will get what resources and how the resulting production of goods and services will be distributed. But market allocation mechanisms have been used effectively within strongly socialist societies where the ownership and control of the means of production are decidedly not private. To be sure, market structures have a predisposition toward private ownership, but it is not an absolute predisposition.

In a similar vein, a socialist system is one in which the means of production are socially or communally controlled and are used to produce goods and services in response to social need. Within socialist systems, central planning has been a principal means for making allocation and investment decisions. But central planning is also a feature of capitalist systems, particularly in the areas of education, defense, transportation infrastructure, and overall policies about growth, inflation, and jobs. Central planning structures have a predisposition toward communal control of the means of production, but it is not an absolute predisposition.

One of the difficulties in comparing capitalism and socialism is that all of the attention has been focused on this distributional side of the equation and little if any has been focused on the production side, the process of getting "from each according to their ability." Both from the perspective of providing for the material welfare of citizens, and that of generating waste products that degrade the environment, production decisions are more important than distribution ones. Even before the breakup in Eastern Europe, capitalist and socialist societies had discovered that neither productivity nor need alone was a particularly good tool for distribution. Thus, capitalist societies all have extensive social safety nets, entitlement programs, and educational systems to ensure that almost everyone can satisfy basic needs regardless of their productive contribution. The tradition of democratic socialism in capitalistic Western Europe is long and deeply held. And socialist societies, even those dominated by authoritarian central governments, have learned that extensive perquisites and noncash rewards—market type incentives—are necessary to get the most out of the "ability" of their citizens. Thus, both kinds of societies depend on incentives to elicit productivity, and both kinds of societies attempt to assure all of their citizens of some reasonable living standard.

Those who are interested in ending, or at least controlling, environmental degradation should be primarily interested in the question of how to create patterns of resource allocation that reflect the needs and interests of a broader community, one that includes not just some, but all contemporary human beings as well as future generations and nature. Thus our next task focuses not on particular ideological choices but rather on how to organize our analyses so that they are instrumental in achieving that communal outcome.

How can economic analysis be organized so as to further the creation of an inclusive community? Economics usually deals with the allocation of scarce resources under some carefully drawn assumptions about human behavior and the availability of resources—individual self-interest and relative scarcity. These assumptions lead economists to think about decision making as a matter of individual autonomy and to see resource scarcity as an opportunity. As a result, economics often lends credence to arguments that paint highly unequal distributions of income as the result of differences in personal productivity. Traditional economic analysis is equally adept at ignoring or trivializing discrimination, class differences, and concentrations of wealth and power.

The facts of economic life, however, begin to make one skeptical about the validity of traditional economic analysis. This is especially true when that analysis is used to try to explain the substantial disparity between the standards of living and the quality of life for those in the small number of industrial nations and those in the rest of the world. A similar skepticism emerges even within particular countries, both poor and rich, when we observe the different conditions under which different groups live. The truth seems to be that for many, existing economic systems in the world provide entrapment, not opportunity; they ensure dependency, not autonomy; and they celebrate the status quo, not innovative and liberating change.

An economist who begins to recognize these realities faces a serious dilemma. The theories provided by traditional economic analysis are elegant, persuasive, and comfortable. Their internal logic is so impeccable, and they can be used so effectively to support the status quo, that it is extremely difficult for a practicing economist to step outside their confines to take a new and different look at the world. But that is precisely the step one must take if one wants to re-view the world and envision a different one from the perspective of the large numbers of people, societies, and species who have been marginalized by the existing world economic order.

Community, Theology, and Power Redefined

It should not be surprising that liberation theologians recognize the Exodus as in some sense an important economic event. The Israelites were marginalized; they were slave labor and the Egyptians used them for their own purposes. The Israelites were not even in a position to offer or withhold their labor, much less bargain in their own interests. The ordering of the society and the distribution of wealth led to an extensive polarization between the rich and the poor. In addition to its obvious religious implications then, the Exodus is also a direct attack on the economic power of an entrenched elite. Liberation theologians are quick to move from the conditions of the Exodus to the consequences of capitalism in the present time. Most of them write in countries that are dependent economically on the concentrations of wealth in countries practicing some form of capitalism. Dependency and domination are "blood sisters." However generous one may want to be with the prevailing global economic order, however reformable one may imagine it capable of becoming, one can hardly deny that it has facilitated an increasing gap between rich nations and poor. The obvious attraction of liberation theologians to socialism is in part driven by an aversion to the consequence of capitalism; but, more intensely, the attraction to socialism is driven by the shift from individual interests to communal interests, which socialism presumes to authorize. Markets certainly can in some ways promote mutuality and reciprocity; indeed, many economists would claim that to be the essence of specialization and exchange. Nevertheless, the elevation of the individual and the tendency toward monopolization of economic power in market economies works against the formation of communities of mutuality. It is not surprising to find that liberation theologians, recognizing that tendency and committed to the preeminence of community, have a borderline addiction to some form of socialism. Even so, while capitalistic markets feature the good of the individual and socialism features the good of community, both are starkly anthropocentric. The ecosystem does not figure in the equation. The question then becomes, How do we imagine an order in which nature is a part of the community?

Some forms of theology in our society—liberal as well as conservative—have focused on the individual and what individuals can do about their destiny and/or their world. Both individual and social salvation can be interpreted as functions of singular initiatives; Billy Graham and Mother Teresa provide alternative and compelling models. Other strains of theology have centered on community and spawned a social ethic. Inadvertently or by design, the symbols of faith have played on the public sphere. And, at least in part, U.S. society has used religious imagery to create and buttress its most enduring societal values. Consequently, we believe that religion and theology have a central role to play in the creation of alternative values and the development of new institutional arrangements. They can enable us to inhabit a different world.

When we consider the ecocrisis, liberation theology does not at first appear to have an obvious role to play; the oppression of nature does not seem as integrally related to our daily lives as human oppression and powerlessness; the central theme of historical liberation in theology does not immediately transfer to the arena of nature. The experience of African Americans, for example, is a natural fit with the Exodus event. The structural similarity between the biblical story and current reality is immediately evident. The two histories line up, and the appeal to God as Liberator connects without straining the imagination. With the environment, however, the problem of the pillage of nature and the affirmations of liberation theology do not immediately fuse, although the existence of environmental racism discloses their proximity. There is no obvious and immediate claim that nature deserves the same epistemological privilege accorded to oppressed human beings. Although one might make the claim that any "theology is necessarily ecological," it is certainly not self-evident that that is so. The case needs to be made explicitly that "love and respect for God involves love and respect for God's creation."[6]

To be sure, the need to relate God and nature, to include creation in the articulation of faith, is not new. Paul Santmire[7] has catalogued the long history of that. The question for liberation theology is whether or not there are any models that can be immediately appropriated. There are at least several in the contemporary theological discussions of the environment that, on their own terms, are impressive. Jay B. McDaniel develops a sense of the immanence of God and represents it through the metaphor "cosmic Heart." "God is that Ultimate life, that cosmic Heart, whose very body is the universe itself."[8] The intrinsic value of nature is in a sense established by a divine impregnation. But what sustains the metaphor is an abstract analysis of process rooted in the philosophy of Whitehead, which is not an attractive starting point for liberation theology. Jürgen Moltmann also engages in an important revaluation of nature through the symbol of "New Creation," which does for nature what "Kingdom of God" does for history.[9] His struggle with an "eschatology of nature" yields an impressive focus on the destiny of the created order. But his support and development of the value of nature convenes more-complex and convoluted arguments than appeal to liberation theologians. Ideas like "the ontological priority of the future" fit the academy better than the streets.

Stewardship is another attempt to revalue nature, utilizing the "love what God loves argument." Herman Daly, an economist and self-identified Christian, argues for responsibility toward "God's World for which we are temporary stewards."[10] Stewardship can be a compelling line of argument and is rooted in the Genesis creation stories Lynn White Jr. distorts. But it can also separate the human species from the rest of creation even as it proposes responsibility; it may recognize a common good, but in human terms only. For liberation theologians, stewardship may be to the environment what charity is to oppression; it can address the result without uncovering the origins of the problem in the systems and institutions of the world. It is an appeal to generosity after the injustice has already occurred.

This cursory survey of some options is not intended to dismiss their significance as ways of advancing the interests of the environment. Its purpose is to assess their congeniality with liberation theology. So, how might liberation theology, on its own terms, address the ecocrisis?

For us, the most congenial work is that of womanist theologians like Karen Baker-Fletcher. When she writes about "caressing of the earth with feet and hands through dance accompanied by the rhythmic syncopation of drums," the image and experience may not resonate with our urban style and accoutrements.[11] But when she speaks of "a wholistic manner" of theology which "remembers God who is the strength of all life . . . and [who] works for the healing and wholeness of creation,"[12] she is within range of our understanding of things. And her determination to break an anthropocentric hold on spirit and see it as embodied in "the rest of creation" is an extension with which we can resonate. When she claims that "the environment . . . must be given the kind of love, nurture, and care that an expectant mother desires for her own body as she looks to . . . the well-being of her developing child,"[13] we are tapping into a sensibility consistent with our arguments for community.

The essential task for us is to facilitate "a re-enchantment of nature"[14] that is freestanding yet converges with central themes in liberation theology. What can it contribute to an irreversible rendering of nature as subject? Clearly, the theology is focused on the objectification of persons in their historical circumstances and is committed to enabling them to be agents in their own history. Paulo Freire[15] also talks about emerging as a subject and learning to act on one's own behalf. We pick up on that theme with the notion of "social heroism," which Weber[16] uses to identify a constituency that consciously rises to its own communal interests. Obviously that idea does not link directly with nature, at least as we are able to perceive it. In a way, nature does achieve its own "voice" as it responds to abuse; yet that is not likely to be the result of a reflective and critical consciousness.

We believe there is a corollary to "social heroism" that can be used in relation to the earth. We have used the term "social heroism" to represent the struggle for human agency in the face of powerlessness. That calls for the creation of a community of mutuality and reciprocity, one where a consciousness of interdependence overrides individualism. What funds our notion of "social heroism" is a deep sense that the components of reality may be distinguishable but are not separable. Then individuals are freed of atomistic views of themselves and dualistic or hierarchical assessments. The reality is that "nothing exists outside relationships";[17] everything that is is within a web. It is tempting to agree with the commonplace assertion that humans stand alone in being accountable. It suggests that human beings have a privileged position and that stewardship is the finest expression of it. But, at heart, it is still anthropocentric. Perhaps we should say instead, "all that we know is inseparable"; reality is seamless. That spawns a holistic approach to the environment in which connection is primary and we resist the temptation to privilege our own reality.

What we are suggesting is that with "social heroism" it is possible to move from a purely human understanding of community to one in which nature is as much a member as we are. Community, then, is a defining hermeneutic. Some would argue that the entry point into a consciousness of connection is rationality; a rational articulation of the problem should be compelling. We are not committed to irrationality but suspect the primacy of reason may imply an "uneven playing field." It's a gift "man has" and leads to themes like stewardship, responsibility, and partnership. Any reconnection of our sensibility with nature will emerge only when we understand ourselves as nature. In Baker-Fletcher's words, we need to understand ourselves as "children of dust and spirit."[18]

Perhaps we do not connect with nature because we do not connect with our own bodies and fail to see them as nature. Particularly in our U.S. culture we see them as objects to be used; both are "other." Moltmann argues that "the rediscovery of external nature will remain incomplete if it is not accompanied by a simultaneous rediscovery of nature 'within'—the nature which the human being is himself, in his bodily makeup."[19] There is a direct connection between our alienation from our bodies and the ecological crisis of our time. It is not surprising that to the degree we objectify our bodies we prevent a view of nature as subject. Because, in Western culture at least, we have devalued our physical bodies, we have also devalued the physical world around us. The abuse of one and the abuse of the other are linked. Conversely, the reconception of ourselves as part of nature may facilitate a more inclusive understanding of community.

In writing about the body/soul relationship Moltmann talks about "a *perichoretic* relationship of mutual interpenetration and differentiated unity"; everything is part of and bound to everything else.[20] That way of viewing "ourselves" precludes the category of primacy and the prospect of domination that follows from it. Without presuming to suggest that the human is normative for all reality, we want to suggest that this understanding is at least paradigmatic. It is often argued that we live in the world we imagine. And what we are claiming is simply that the imagination of ourselves as "mutual interpenetration and differentiated unity" authorizes such a perichoretic vision of "everything" in ways that foreclose privilege. If none are privileged in creation, then all are subjects. We are simple "interbeings among inter-beings."[21]

On the surface at least, it would appear there is a tension between the preservation of subject status for everything and the exercise of power. And it is difficult to imagine a sociopolitical environment in which power is exorcised. Some sense of power and some use of power would seem to be necessary conditions for significant change, indeed for life. We are tempted to argue that power got us where we are in the ecocrisis and power will be required to move us beyond it. This is always a particularly vexing issue for liberation theologians, who know that oppression is a function of domination, being overpowered; at the same time, they are well aware that achieving subject status is compromised when the oppressed must plead in some form for their freedom. Exercising the claim, "by any means necessary," is often the only way for the victims to move the oppressors. The use of "Black Power" did penetrate the numbness of white America.

Now when the issues are formed around the reality of power, liberation theologies suffer some ambiguity. On the one hand, it is clear that the oppressed are in that condition because some group—often small—is able to define the conditions of existence for other groups through the systems and institutions of the social order. Whether it is "First World" over "Third World," white over person of color, male over female, or straight over gay, the plight of the victim is sustained by the simple fact of sovereign control and mastery in some form. On the other hand, it does take power to break the chains of oppression. There is no common grace that periodically infects the privileged and teases them into the posture of generosity. The Israelites would still be in bondage if they waited for the Egyptians to be overcome by goodwill! There is rarely any liberation without some invocation of power or at least the threat of it. Liberation theologians are particularly uncomfortable with that response, precisely because power is the weapon of the oppressors. Exercising power means risking contamination by it. One is so readily drawn into the very distorted processes of the oppressors. The prospect of a new bondage is real. Theologians and others are quite right when they note it's a question of both who has the power and what sort of power. We need a notion of power that is not controlled by individual self-interest achieved through domination.

One way to contextualize the paradox of the need for and the fear of power is to think about the middle class in the United States. They are locked in a "tri-lemma," in which general economic conditions leave them vulnerable to poverty, their low-level participation in corporate cost-cutting may make them culpable for the poverty of others, and they are powerless to change either condition.[22] Those of us in the middle class have relatively little control over the conditions of our lives and individually cannot withstand or resist a rapidly deteriorating position for either ourselves or others. That reality is well documented in a recent book by Barbara Ehrenreich titled *The Fear of Falling: The Inner Life of the*

Middle Class. The same powerlessness prevails in relation to the environment. By and large we do not personally create and cannot change our environmental conditions. Individual members of the middle class have, at best, a nominal ability to influence things. These conditions in our society result from decisions that are made within institutions that have economic, political, and social power. Those realities are marked by domination, mastery, and exploitation and the fostering of the institutions that embody them. Our alternatives call for a cooperative undertaking marked by reciprocity and solidarity. It is a "social heroism" in that the interests of the commonweal, the common good, have priority and the institutions that implement them are to be free of domination. In this framework the environment is a partner in its own right, upon which we are dependent and for which we are responsible. That is the essence of reciprocity: mutual interdependence and responsibility. To establish the reciprocity requires us to recognize that the environment is not just something "there for us" but matters in itself.

For liberation theologians the ambiguity of power is in part eased by the innocence of the oppressed; and here the analysis fits because the innocence of nature is self-evident. Liberation theology has always argued that we begin with a conscious preference for those who are victims. In one sense, of course, all of nature, including humans, are victimized by environmental degradation; there are no clear winners and losers. But the determination of who absorbs the costs contributes to victimization. As we suggested with the electricity production example in chapter 1, in our economy the most vulnerable will pay the most because they have the least ability to protect their interests. Among humans, the most vulnerable will be the economic underclass and racial and ethnic minorities; but nature itself is also vulnerable in that case, as the impact of acid rain shows.

Liberation theology leads us to enter the environmental dilemma we have described with our attention focused on those who have little or no choice. Thus, it would be unacceptable to let the burden of environmentally induced unemployment be borne by a single segment of U.S. society. Siding with the choiceless means refusing to accept any solutions that are achieved on the backs of the lower classes. Solidarity with the potentially unemployed is the place to be. The innocence of those persons is not grounded in any inherent righteousness or virtue, but simply in the fact that they have no power to use in the protection of their interests. Their goal is survival, not greed. And so the powerless in their powerlessness escape at least some of the forms of perversity to which the privileged have abundant access. And the use of power on their behalf, shaped by mutuality and reciprocity, can be free of domination.

One of the dimensions of liberation theology that has made it consequential in the sphere of history is the essential equation of salvation and liberation. One's destiny with God is linked with action on behalf of justice. "To know God is to do justice" loads the divine reality into acts in solidarity with the victims. God is where freedom is. Put another way, one's salvation is at risk in one's responses to the injustices of the global order. Being one with God and being in solidarity with the victim may not be identical but they are inseparable. That raises the stakes immeasurably. If I am not responsive to who and what is getting hurt, my link with God is broken. Now we have established through our illustration of electricity and the consequences of its production that the environment and the spheres of our historical existence interlock and interpenetrate. When we affirm the inseparability of salvation and liberation we are claiming that our responses to the environment are of a piece with our relationship with the God of justice. We put our salvation at risk in exploiting the earth, for it is "a God-infused and God-breathed place."[23] While McFague sets the issue with the image that the world is "God's Body," liberation theology needs to argue that to live in mutuality and solidarity with the earth is to know God, not because God is earth but because God is inseparable from a liberated earth just as God is inseparable from a liberated people.

Liberation theology is written from the historically particular and concrete. Its first word is always one that articulates the human condition of oppression. Its matrix is the struggle to be free. It is so unique and powerful in marshaling resistance to exploitation in part because of the degree to which it fuses the themes of creation, salvation, and liberation. Mainstream theology has tended to consider them "in order" and as if separate; at some point there may be a disposition to draw connections. Liberation theologians see the three themes as distinguishable in impulse but not separable in meaning. One of the driving and defining events for liberation theologians is the Exodus. And the Exodus is the means by which we interpret creation, salvation, and liberation. Creation is understood as the first installment in the drama of salvation. It is not to be conceived of as a separate event that provides the setting for history. Creation is included in salvation and as such "is the work of the Redeemer."[24] God the Redeemer creates! That may be good news for history, but it does not ensure that nature will be understood as subject. Salvation has as its goal communion with God, but what is unique is that it is a preeminently historical solidarity. The community of faith is one with God in doing justice. And the content of the salvic work is liberation, setting free of all persons from domination by alien forces. To say that one's salvation is near at hand is to say that the promise of freedom is about to be realized. But the promise of the earth is subordinate when creation is understood as the initiation of a historical process. That is, the historical process is paramount in this view, and nature provides little more than the setting.

For Gustavo Gutiérrez, creation, salvation, and liberation have as their focus the creation of "a new humanism, one in which man is defined first of all by his responsibility toward his brother and toward history."[25] The intent of the God of justice is a "new man" in a new community of people. Creation, salvation, liberation have a social setting; they require a new ordering of life, a new conception of the common good. "To work, to transform this world, is to become a man and to build a human community; it is also to save. Likewise, to struggle against misery and exploitation and to build a just society is already to be a part of the saving action."[26] Thus, the outcome is a new society of mutual empowering, where the well-being of the whole is the matrix for individual enrichment, in which the structure and systems facilitate freedom and preempt domination. The unmistakable contribution of liberation theology has been to invest the full reality of the Divine in the concrete realities of life, which are threatened by death in all its forms. Thus, the Exodus is the cipher for understanding the full scope of God's agency and fusing it to the present condition of oppression. And that "works" when one's present realities are historical exploitation, but it is startlingly anthropocentric. The oppression of nature is not visible on the scene. Nature may be conspicuously evident in the Exodus stories but not in a way that would lead one to understand its rights. Its status, once again, is only that of the setting for the drama of God's liberating work in history.

It is commonplace to argue that the ecocrisis is a side effect of the striving of humans for power and domination. It is unfortunate that this search for power often gets theological support with metaphors of the all-powerful God in whose image humans are made. Many theologians affirm a notion of power that has been liberated from domination. This is not "unilateral power" but "relational power."[27] Some speak of it as a "power with" rather than a "power over." Relational power will not tolerate any diminishment of the other; indeed, its goal is to empower. And this is a vision of power that is observable in much of nature, both the human and the nonhuman. Human beings, in their interpersonal relationships, often strive for mutual and reciprocal empowerment. That characterizes marriages and teaching at their best. Within the broader reality of nature, symbiotic relationships provide dramatic support for the importance of mutuality and reciprocity. Such relationships do not use and abuse but rather build and reinforce. So empowering nature need not seem so fanciful. It is precisely the history of *controlling* nature for our purposes alone that has created our crisis; it is our working *against* nature that has made the environment less habitable. To empower nature does not mean to let it *alone* but to let it *be*, to build with it a reciprocal relationship that mutually enhances us as a part of nature and nature as a part of us.

We have suggested elsewhere that our images for God have consequences. The metaphor of liberator for God is obviously crucial in our theology and has implications for historical oppression. But it is not so clear how the image of liberator functions in relation to nature. It can play on humankind and its disposition to control and dominate others, to exploit and impoverish, but can the image impact and influence the subject status of the environment? Jürgen Moltmann argues that there are "two archetypal images of liberation: the Exodus and the sabbath."[28] The Exodus from bondage in Egypt, where the Israelites were slave labor, to the promised land is a symbol representing the action of God in history. God intervenes in the social, economic, and political setting of God's people. Now, "the sabbath is the elemental experience of God's creation, . . . the God who is and is present."[29] Having made the world as God's home and our inheritance, God rests on the seventh day. The sabbath symbolizes the freedom within, the quiet and rest from labor. "By coming to his rest, God lets his creation [all of it] be what it is on its own."[30] On the sabbath God experiences what God has created. God enters into a unique relationship with God's creation. A spectacular closeness emerges. Again in Moltmann's words, "he feels the world, he allows himself to be affected, to be touched by each of his creatures. He adopts the community of creation as his own milieu."[31] In a symbolic sense, history begins with God's resting and receiving the world. It is the beginning of God and the world's history with each other.

On the sabbath the creation is celebrated as subject by the divine subject. For Moltmann the sabbath and the Exodus are integrally related; they complement each other. The internal freedom of the sabbath and the external freedom of the Exodus require each other. Peace in God's presence and the rendering humane of the world are indivisible. God's creation sabbath and God's historical Exodus are symbols for resisting objectification; they "free all to be what it is." God the liberator provides the model of the promised future for both history and nature.

Community, Mutual Interests, and Economic Institutions

While we have argued that religion and theology can play a significant role in shaping societal values, economic institutions often form the structures that define the organization of society. The earlier debate between socialism and capitalism pivots on that reality. The immediate issue before us once again is one that centers on the inclusion of nature as one dimension of community. But that falls in the realm of values; inclusion is necessary but not sufficient. Making inclusion effective requires the creation of mediating and sustaining structures.

It is one thing to *say* that we must "free all to be what it is." It is much more difficult to create the conditions that make that happen. We want to suggest some of the institutional and structural changes that might allow the creation of an economic system that recognizes nature, as well as current and future generations of human beings, as significant actors with subject status who interact with each other in a "community of mutual interests." In effect, we are asking whether it is possible to create such a community, which extends beyond the human and the contemporary. We can approach the issue somewhat obliquely by exploring the possible characteristics of such a community and then propose policies that elicit the development of those characteristics.

As we think about characteristics, it is useful to begin by remembering one of the principal purposes of any economic system—the allocation of scarce resources to satisfy potentially unlimited wants. Scarcity is a central fact; economics exists because the members of a community want more than is available. In a community shaped by mutuality, the recognition of scarcity ought to extend to the environment as well and lead to a reduction in material throughput. A smaller amount of waste product would leave for future generations an ecosystem that had cleaner air and water and was aesthetically more pleasing. It would also put less pressure on the survival of nonhuman species that are threatened by pollution.

A second characteristic also focuses on the "mutual" in our community of mutual interests. If we assume, as traditional economists do, that individuals typically seek their own self-interest, then it is necessary to create a communal structure in which self-interest is informed by, infused with, and thus serves communal interest. To accomplish that, it will be necessary to move away from the situation in which the present generation of elite in the industrial world has a virtual monopoly on the choices about resource use. Empowering the poor, people of color, women, future generations, and nature means allowing them to play an effective role in deciding on appropriate patterns of current resource use.

The emergence of these characteristics does not necessarily entail a complete change in the mode of economic analysis; using the market as a tool to allocate scarce resources can still serve the desirable goal of efficiency. That is ultimately what markets do. The often unasked question is, "efficiency to do what?" In the 1930s Joseph Schumpeter detailed the central role of the entrepreneur in bringing about growth and change in a capitalist market economy.[32] The entrepreneur sees an opportunity for profit and responds with an innovation. We believe that it is possible to shape the institutional arrangements in the society so that entrepreneurs will envision opportunity in the implementation of ecologically appropriate innovation.[33] Economics shows us that prices and profits can and do move resources. What is needed is a technique to make prices move us toward reduced use of materials, and a technique to make the price system reflect the interests of those, human and other, who have been marginalized by the existing system.

One possibility rests with the implementation of a coordinated set of policies designed to establish institutions whose actions are constrained by limits on economic growth. Herman Daly refers to this as creating a "steady state."[34] While the immediate creation of a steady state is not necessarily optimal, it would be better than the current growth-oriented conditions in terms of the sustainability of the conditions for well-being. It also, de facto, recognizes at least some rights for future generations, since ending current growth slows down the use of resources and therefore leaves more resources for use by future generations.

Daly proposes an institutional arrangement to control income distribution and limit wealth accumulation, an institution to control population growth, and an institution to assure the sustainable use of resources.[35] Control of income is necessary in order both to limit the amount of consumption, and thus economic growth, and to establish the conditions of equity that allow each person to be an actor with some power to affect his or her own condition. A negative income tax with both a minimum and a maximum income level per individual or family would help to achieve this goal. Too little income means needs go unmet; too much income confers too much power. An income maximum also limits the possibilities for accumulation of wealth. The use of the negative income tax as the tool for accomplishing this places the actual after-tax income distribution under the control of the market, thus leaving in place *some* economic incentive for the pursuit of individual excellence, that is, greater productivity will generate greater income. The tax system should allow some of that income to accrue to the earner so as to encourage productivity growth.

A wealth and inheritance tax system would limit the amount of wealth accumulation. This is a much more controversial idea, since it infringes on our notions of individual rights to private property. Nevertheless, it is necessary if we want to sustain income limits; wealth is a major source of income. Wealth from inheritance confers power to control and consume resources without any contribution of personal productivity. Thus one generation's income and pattern of resource use could be well within sustainability limits, while the second generation's behavior could violate those limits because of excessive consumption supported by inherited wealth. This outcome can be especially pernicious if, as is the case in much of the world, the initial distribution of wealth favors the industrialized world and, even within countries, advantages some on the basis of race, gender, and class.

A second set of institutional structures involves the creation of a method to reduce population growth to zero.[36] The rationale for this is that sustaining any standard of living with a growing population requires a growing level of output and resource use. The only way to respond to that is to reduce fertility to the replacement level. Once again, the preferred method for accomplishing this relies on the market, using Kenneth Boulding's idea of transferable birth licenses assigned to each woman.[37] Those licenses would be sellable in the open market, ensuring that those who wanted more than 2.1 children (replacement level fertility) could have them if they were willing to pay the market price to buy extra licenses from those who wanted fewer than 2.1 children. This idea sounds and probably is extreme; it is also a good example of creating a situation in which the market still acts as the allocation mechanism for resources but the outcome from the market action is very different. Every market solution works within the limits imposed by the initial availability and allocation of resources. Boulding's proposal simply changes the initial amount and the allocation of fertility resources and then allows the market to decide who actually uses those resources. The idea seems perhaps to favor the rich and to move ethical decision making into the crass arena of the market, but we need to remember that if income and wealth distribution mechanisms are put in place, they will limit the power of the rich. And as Daly argues, "It is not the exchange relationship that debases life. . . . It is the underlying inequity in wealth and income beyond any functional or ethical justification that loads the terms of free [market] exchange against the poor."[38]

The third area of institutional creation involves responding to the depletion of resources that is a natural result of economic activity.[39] That depletion could be reduced and controlled by means of an auction of resource quotas. The buyers in the auction would be those who wish to use resources, e.g., producers of consumer goods who need energy resources in their production process. Armed with their purchased quota rights, these producers would then be able to buy resources from private resource owners at market-determined prices. Thus the producers would first have to buy quotas and then buy the resources. The ultimate price for using resources should be raised by this two-tiered market for purchasing their use. That will both discourage the use of depletable resources and encourage the substitution of alternative renewable, or at least more abundant, resources.

The rationale here is that it is much easier to control pollution by using fewer resources than by producing less waste.[40] And, once again, limiting the use of resources preserves their availability for future generations. To ensure that outcome, Daly suggests that quotas be set so that renewable resources would be used at some level at or below the maximum sustainable yield. For nonrenewable resources the quota should be small enough to ensure a total resource price at least as high as the price of the nearest renewable substitute, thus encouraging the use of renewable substitutes. When there are no substitutes, quotas would have to reflect some ethical judgment about the appropriate distribution of use between present and future generations.[41] An important caveat here is that the existing distribution of resources confers power, and that affects who gets to use what resources. Limiting the overall use of resources, but allowing their allocation to depend on existing distributions of power, is simply another way to load the cost of environmental degradation onto those who are already disadvantaged.

The policy and institution-building approach outlined above would move us a long way toward sustainability and hence some sort of intergenerational equity in our use of the biosphere. But it still puts things in those terms, "use of the biosphere," and thus continues to treat nature as an object for use and control. There are two additional policy/institutional choices that might help to achieve subject status for nature. The first would be to extend the idea of depletion quotas and set those quotas at such a level that no plant or animal species would be destroyed by an avoidable human-induced reduction in the resource base. That would move us from sustainability viewed from a purely human perspective to sustainability as a biospheric norm. In part, that means that environmental amenities—clean air, water, aesthetics—would be treated as depletable resources subject to quota.

The extension of the depletion quotas ought to be reinforced by a movement to put real teeth into an "Endangered Species Act," adding many more plant species as well as animal species to the list. As the current act is usually interpreted and enforced, it largely focuses on the survival of animal species, but does little to ensure the long-term viability of those species, and it does nothing for plant species unless they are necessary for the survival of an animal species. In a sense, the current act tries to ensure the survival of species, but it does little to ensure the appropriate functioning of those species within the ecological system. Such a move, it seems to us, would be an essential part of any effort to "free all to be what it is." It is the "freeing all" that creates the richness and diversity that builds a truly sustainable biosphere.

Up to this point we have suggested both new institutional arrangements and new kinds of economic analysis that might empower the marginalized, dramatically reduce the destructive differences in economic well-being that characterize the existing conditions, and prevent the reemergence of concentrated economic wealth and power. For example, we have called for cooperative and communal decision making that recognizes the economic interests of all; we have also suggested limits on the aggregation and inheritance of wealth; and we have recommended other policy changes that would affect biodiversity and the use of depletable resources.

None of these proposals, on their surface, would necessarily have a positive impact on the problem of environmental degradation. As our electricity production example in chapter 1 pointed out, traditional economic analysis places ecological concerns in a group of problems identified as "externalities." Those are situations where normal private economic decision making leads to an outcome in which there are serious side effects from the production and consumption of a product. If the side effects are not accounted for in the usual cost/price signals that the market uses to direct resources into or away from the production of certain goods, then we are said to incur social cost or, occasionally, receive social benefits. Pollution problems are social cost problems. Most economists would contend that such problems arise because of an improperly functioning market, one that does not effectively account for the relative scarcity of various environmental resources. And the major cause of malfunction, they claim, is a lack of clearly defined property rights: since no one owns the air, no one has a vested financial interest in using their productive resources to sustain its quality; there are no obvious price signals to which the society can respond. Solutions, for most economists, would involve increasing privatization and marketization of the decision-making process. In other words, find some mechanism to assign property rights to environmental amenities. That will allow price signals to work and encourage the owners to use those amenities, to allocate their relative scarcity, in an efficient and welfare-creating manner.

Recently, some economists have begun to suggest that environmental problems may arise as much from absolute resource scarcity as from poorly defined property rights. We have already alluded to their focus on sustainability in Daly's analysis of the "steady state" and the associated proposals for institutional reform. These economists call for a current set of production and consumption decisions, which would allow for "sustainable" development. This means a level of economic activity that draws upon the existing limited resource base in such a way that that level of activity can be sustained into the indefinite future. Thus, not only must our economic institutions respond to the economic needs of the current generation, but they must also be structured in such a way that the needs of future generations can be adequately represented in the decision-making process. Obviously, such an approach to determining the level and mix of economic activity calls for analysis, policy prescriptions, and institution building that are much more intrusive than those of traditional economics.

Maintenance of the quality and diversity of the ecosphere, however, ultimately demands an analysis and a set of policy choices that are not anthropocentric. Can we develop a claim for changing our economic analysis from one that views nature and its resources as things to be used by human beings to one in which nature is viewed as a participant in the process, with intrinsic rights of its own? In our terminology, this view identifies nature as a category of analysis.

We have alluded to some of our earlier work in which we argued that the poor, the disadvantaged, the marginalized, and even the middle class are essentially powerless and have very little ability to affect the structure and the outcome of the economic decision-making process. We made the case for new systemic arrangements that stress mutuality and reciprocity. That is a way of calling for a change in the boundary conditions, the constraints or limits within which the economic system must operate at any given time. In that analysis we thought it necessary to create some new constraints by changing both the initial allocation of resources—*who has what at the start*—and the social goals inherent in the process of economic decision making—*what should we do with the resources we have?* If we want to respond to the ecocrisis, then those boundary conditions, the setting in which social systems operate, must be further modified by extending the time frame for analysis and by expanding membership in the decision-making process to include the ecological system in which we are all embedded. Unless our notions of mutuality and reciprocity are extended to encompass those not related to us temporally and as well as nature itself, no set of economic and social decision-making processes can achieve sustainability or moderate significantly the ecocrisis.

We contend that there is a viable and important place for nature in the community of mutual interests that we believe is claimed by God as liberator. Such a community seems a natural extension of the history-centered analysis of liberation theology. Just as the end of human oppression and the restoration of subject status for all humans begins in an analysis of the historical conditions of oppression, so too does the end of the degradation of nature begin with an analysis of the historical conditions that generated the objectification of nature, the instrumental approach that encouraged "use" to become "abuse."

Many of those historical conditions have arisen because of choices made within economic systems about the use of natural resources. Therefore, the development of a "liberation economics" as a tool for analyzing those conditions seems appropriate. The economic institution building that we suggest, drawing upon Daly as a starting point, provides an argument for the feasibility of that development. Changing the human economic institutions would reduce the human impact on the environment, opening up the possibility for patterns of reciprocal use that are sustainable for all parts of nature, including human beings. Implementation would begin to create the conditions that would ensure a viable existence for *all* human beings, the spotted owl, and the northwest forests one hundred years from now.

T·H·R·E·E

Economics and the Common Good

One cannot think of community, and begin to liberate oneself and one's discipline from individualism, without bringing into focus the question of "the common good." While some may have an intuitive commitment to that good, most of us come to consider it only when we experience its absence, at least in relation to the environment. A decade ago it would not have occurred to the residents of Granville to form a "Committee for the Common Good." It took the stealthlike advance of blacktop and the threat of well-financed commercial developers to bring some citizens to create such a body. Violation of the common good may be the trigger that calls it to our attention.

Our two disciplines have a different journey in relation to claims about the social welfare. The common good is not a first-order consideration for most economists; to be sure, they talk about it, but only as a by-product of their methodology. It is not usual for economists to think of the welfare of the society as in any way different from the sum of individual well-being. Theologians, on the other hand, frequently take it as a category of analysis. The defects in their process begin to emerge with the question "the common good for whom?" Who gets to define it and who or what is counted and valued are not arenas of innocence. As often as not the lens is narrow; at best, it is that of an elite and powerful group that "notices" the victims. And that is especially the case in relation to the environment.

In *State of the World 1991,* Lester R. Brown notes that we are now living in a time when "the battle over ideology" between the East and the West has been replaced by "the battle to save the planet."[1] The difference between the Cold War struggle and the environmental one is that in the former the goal was to transform the values and actions of our antagonists, while in the latter winning involves transforming our own values and actions.[2] As we think about that agenda, Brown observes, there is a striking difference between the viewings of an economist and an ecologist. While economists see some significant burdens, they seem "manageable" in the long term; for ecologists, "the situation could hardly be worse."[3] Brown contends that "every major indicator shows a deterioration in natural systems: forests are shrinking, deserts are expanding, croplands are losing topsoil, the stratospheric ozone layer continues to thin, greenhouse gases are accumulating, the number of plant and animal species is diminishing, air pollution has reached health-threatening levels in hundreds of cities, and damage from acid rain can be seen on every continent."[4]

Unfortunately, the intellectual worlds of the economist and the ecologist rarely touch in ways that are consequential for the economic system. Economic theory and practice seldom address the scale factors necessary to understand the carrying capacity of the planet. Most economists do not relate to the intricate interaction of systems so crucial to the ecologist but instead blithely extrapolate from the recent past toward a promising future. The pursuit of growth, "more is better," is assumed to be such an indisputable "good" that its consequences to the natural order seldom enter the equation. The irony is that this schizoid ignoring of nature in order to promote growth will inevitably lead to the very economic collapse that economists wish to avoid.[5]

Theology shares with economics a similar blindness to including the natural order as a participant in the common good. Protestantism in particular, with its emphasis on grace coming to human beings in a human form, enabled nature to become "the ward of science and technology."[6] Theologians often abandoned nature as a location of divine activity because science conceived of the natural order as having its own, internally logical processes. Some of us would want to suggest that this dismissal of nature has been driven by a need to avoid functioning in what, at times, has been considered the war zone between science and religion. Oliver argues that the rejection of a theology of nature was in fact willful; "the failure to 'thematize nature' was intentional."[7] Some theologians hoped that a retreat from nature would place religion in a secure sphere free of challenge.

Prior to the 1960s, when environmental issues became prominent, theologians engaged in their own schizophrenia, one that sustained an obsession with history rather than nature. Oliver quotes Bultmann as a self-conscious example: "Our relationship to history is wholly different from our relationship to nature. Man, if he rightly understand himself, differentiates himself from nature. When he observes nature, he perceives there something objective which is not himself. When he turns his attention to history, however, he must admit himself to be a part of history."[8] For us, it is difficult to imagine any validity to a claim that we are not a part of nature. But whatever the reasons or relationships, both economic theory and theology have usually functioned as if the natural order were no disciplinary concern of theirs.

Our agenda as a theologian and an economist is to join the separated, to attempt as others have in the last few decades to include nature in our disciplinary and interdisciplinary work. Unlike Bultmann, we want to claim that distinctions between the orders of history and nature cannot be sustained. Indeed, we are shaped by and we have shaped both realms. Nature and history meet in us and we meet in them. Our goal is to include that fact about nature in transformed economic and theological analyses. In this chapter we will be concerned more explicitly with economics.

Sustainability as a New Regard for Nature

When economists do have a vision of community that includes nature, the common good is often addressed through the concept of sustainability, which argues against sacrificing the future for present growth. And sustainability means that any level of human activity on the planet is viable only as long as it places a small enough load on the use of resources that the quality, diversity, and ability to provide services from the ecosphere can be maintained at at least the existing level for an indefinite future. Thus space and time are connected irrevocably. The issue of sustainability is only now emerging within the widespread multidisciplinary examination of the environment. Neither theology nor economics, as disciplines, has been in the vanguard of that examination. In different ways, practitioners of the two disciplines have been "in denial." The natural order is a project theologians have often avoided and economists ignored; the mission of responding to nature's claims for restraint has not intruded upon our methodological consciousness.

The prevailing values and institutions that dominate our society and the world are not set up for maintaining or even addressing sustainability. In developing his metaphor of the "spaceship earth," Kenneth Boulding[9] likens our existing conditions within the world economic system to behavior consistent with the expansion of the frontier in U.S. history. He identifies that as the "cowboy" economy, dependent on the assumption that there is always more land, more resources, and an unlimited possibility for expansion. In that cowboy economy the disposal of waste products is seen as so small a factor relative to the absorptive capacity of the ecosphere that no one worries about pollution or environmental degradation. Sustainability is seen not as a problem to be addressed but as a given assured by enormous abundance. The resources available to provide for the common good are effectively without limit.

The cowboy metaphor has been at least tacitly supported by both theologians and economists, often in service to individualism. Theologians have been intent on confining the description and analysis of the faith to human history rather than the natural order; economists have been dazzled by the analytic attractiveness of market models built on relative rather than absolute scarcity. It is only recently in either discipline that serious attention has been given to broader-based ecological concerns such as sustainability.

In a way, the issue we are raising here involves a broadening of the questions addressed by environmental racism. That analysis contends that both the incidence of environmental degradation and the attempts to redress it impose a heavy burden on the groups in society, the underclass and racial and ethnic minorities, who are least able to bear the burden and least able to defend themselves against it. So production activity that generates environmental externalities is much more likely to be located in geographic areas populated by the poor, African Americans, and other disadvantaged groups. And attempts to "clean up" will either involve treatment facilities like the East Liverpool incinerator or reductions in production activities that lead to unemployment. In both cases, the impact is felt in a differentially heavy way by the poor and disadvantaged.

We argue that it is possible and appropriate to add nature to the groups disadvantaged by externalities. The cowboy economy does create social costs, diseconomies that reduce the well-being of relatively powerless human beings in society. But it also tears apart the ecological base that supports and sustains nonhuman species' diversity. And so, a powerless nature is damaged by this activity in much the same way as disadvantaged and powerless human beings. The two effects are the same, and until we generate a sustainability that recognizes both sets of damage, we are unlikely to seriously ameliorate either.

Our own economic analysis has focused on ways to tempt the market to distribute goods and services more fairly, and to address the desperate needs of those who have been left out. That is always a problematic endeavor because economics tends to be ahistorical; it imagines that there are universal laws that govern decision making about the allocation and use of resources. Only in a few areas, such as development economics, are some practitioners driven to wonder how supposedly universal laws could possibly generate such incredible differences in material well-being. That leads some economists to move from the ahistorical universal theory to the historical circumstances of societies as a way to explain what the laws cannot. For these economists, the goal is to explore ways of forming new institutional arrangements and a new history in which the poor and oppressed have greater access to the necessities of life.

Our liberation-based theological analysis has been concerned with a new history as well, one in which the subjugated become subjects. The weight of the Judeo-Christian tradition is in solidarity with the rising up of those who have been driven down. Now our shared goal is to explore whether the same themes can help push our disciplines in the direction of valuing nature, moving away from our common blindness, allowing nature's voice to be heard in the way our disciplines do their analyses, and including it in our notion of community.

To return for a moment to a theme we introduced in the last chapter, the real issue in building a sustainable society is not whether the society is more market-oriented or more socialistically oriented. The issue is not the political/economic system, but rather the pattern of resource utilization that arises. Does it serve the common good in the broadest sense? There is little doubt that the consumption of goods and services is one important component of the world's environmental problem. And the distribution of income that fuels that consumption is clearly unequal in all societies. There probably is some degree of inequality necessary to sustain incentives in most societies. That is, getting "from each according to his ability" requires some differential rewards in order to elicit productive contributions in line with ability. On the other hand, extreme inequality is seen as an injustice and that fuels increased societal discord, not greater productivity. That is even truer when the inequality is correlated with race, ethnicity, and gender.

In addition, extreme inequality seems also to lead to inequality and inefficiency in the use of environmental resources. U.S. energy consumption is clearly extravagant compared to that of the rest of the world. In 1991, we accounted for more than 25 percent of the world's energy consumption; on a per capita basis, we consumed at a rate more than five times the world average. We can "afford it" because of an inordinately large share of the world's income and consumption ability. U.S. unwillingness to cooperate fully in the "earth summits" of the 1990s reflects our concern about sacrificing any of our current levels of consumption of the earth's resources. Turning around that attitude demands reduced inequality, and that pushes us in the direction of a more "communal" distribution system. But notice here that "more communal" simply means a distribution system that has less inequality and more concern for need; it does not suggest anything about the specific form of the distribution system. And, of course, it focuses only on the human use of resources without considering the interests of the natural order that yields them.

The most extreme environmental problems and the largest failures with pure market economies do not, however, arise on the distribution side of the market. Indeed, distribution and consumption seem to be afterthoughts when we explore the real sources of power in the economic and political setting. It is production decisions that control which resources will be used and how they will be used. If those decisions produce goods and services that don't serve the needs of the underclass, and that damage the viability of the ecosphere, then no amount of post-production redistribution will solve the problem. The current move toward market-dominated economic decision making does not ensure that environmental resources will be used more efficiently in the service of the human community. It only ensures that resources will be used efficiently in the service of the elite who own and/or control the means of production. The goals of that elite are more likely to involve maintenance and extension of their own power than careful sustenance of the earth's resources. There is no a priori reason why they would concern themselves with the well-being either of disadvantaged human beings or of nature. That adds one more economic factor to the generation of ecocrisis. Twentieth-century history would suggest that environmental decay emerges because the process of industrial growth ignores the possibility of absolute scarcity, ignores the needs of future generations, ignores the needs of the poor and powerless, and ignores the interests of nonhuman species.

If, indeed, none of those needs and interests can be completely represented in a market economy, then environmental demands create an imperative for communal as opposed to individual decision making. Environmental demands do call for an economic system that uses resources efficiently; using environmental resources profligately is what has gotten us into our current fix. Within limits, efficiency is more likely to occur when market processes are used to allocate those resources. More efficient allocation of resources is one of the driving forces behind the historical development of both the practice and theory of the market. But the market cannot make a decision, for example, that a 90 percent reduction in carbon dioxide emissions is necessary for the health of the biosphere; that is a communal decision. Once such a decision about scale is made, the next desirable goal is to accomplish the 90 percent reduction in such a way as to interfere as little as possible with the production of goods and services. Some resources previously devoted to goods production will now have to be used for emission reduction. The secondary goal ought to be to accomplish the primary goal of 90 percent emission reduction using the fewest resources possible. That might mean some producers reduce emissions 60 percent and others 98 percent. The market is a powerful tool for making that allocation decision. But even then, without the competitive forces that Adam Smith envisioned, concentrations of monopoly power within a market economy or political power within an authoritarian system lead to narrow allocation decisions that do not represent the interests of the society at large.

The new political/economic institutions that characterize a sustainable economy have to create a set of limitations for the market that prevent concentrations of economic power. At the same time, the process of creating, changing, and sustaining those new institutions must be a process that includes and is founded upon the widest possible communal involvement. One of the ways of doing this would be to have a largely market allocation system for an economy that is embedded in a largely socialist political system.

The complex problem of energy consumption can illustrate this new synthesis. Fossil fuel energy resources are relatively scarce. Their burning creates carbon dioxide and other chemical waste products, which contribute to smog, acid rain, ozone depletion, and global warming. Historically, we have used the price system to allocate those resources. The traditional market argument has been that rising prices for those resources will make it profitable both to conserve existing resources and to search for alternatives, either of which would reduce the environmental impact. But the existing concentrations of economic and political power have pushed us in the direction of overvaluing fossil sources of energy and undervaluing the damage they do to the environment. The result has been that the rising prices have not moved us at all rapidly toward substitutes; prices have not risen rapidly enough. In addition, the concentration of economic power in the hands of fossil fuel energy producers has restricted the flow of resources and financing toward the development of technologically feasible substitutes. So even if we as individuals want to shift our own energy consumption patterns away from fossil fuels and toward cleaner and more abundant alternatives like solar energy, the technological infrastructure necessary to support our decision does not exist. Ecological economists identify this as a "lock-in" problem; that is, we are, as a society, locked into a pattern of energy use that is not in our best long-term interests because some historical choices about technology make it too expensive for most of us to shift to alternatives. The electricity production example we used in chapter 1 is an illustration of this. Our existing technology for electricity generation locks us in to production that is both large-scale and dependent on fossil fuels.

The situation is not significantly different in socialist societies. East Liverpool, Ohio, can happen anywhere. While socialism may pay greater lip service to the common good, that good is still narrowly defined. Prior to its breakup, the Soviet Union relied very heavily on fossil fuels as energy sources. The environmental damage arising from that reliance has been extensive, both locally and globally. In other words, the same overvaluing/undervaluing problem existed there. There too, the energy administrators played a powerful role within the central planning authority and were thus important political players. The results in terms of substitutes and new technology have been just the same as in the capitalist societies. This suggests once again that the real culprits are industrial growth and concentrated decision-making power, with particular political and economic systems perhaps exacerbating the problem, but not causing it. What we need more than anything else is a new set of values that deemphasize anthropocentric economic growth as a good per se and focus instead on improving the overall quality of life for all life forms. To use but one example, imagine that we had a universally held value that favored recycling of waste products. Not only would such a value inspire an ethical commitment to recycling, it would also generate the economic incentives to create a recycling system. That is, the widespread commitment would generate the demand that would make the system work. Building a sustainable ecosystem is absolutely dependent on the emergence of that kind of value system, one where the vision of the common good encompasses the natural order, and that in turn leads to the creation of economic institutions that support the common good and liberate both humans and nature.

A New Economic Paradigm

The creation of this liberation economics requires establishing a new paradigm centered on achieving the common good. Its focus would be transposing economic analysis from the ahistorical to the historical and from the anthropocentric to the naturocentric. Whatever the paradigm for economic analysis, all economists recognize that their "science" is about allocating scarce resources to meet unlimited wants. We already claimed in chapter 1 that economics exists because people want more than is available. Most economic analysis has been grounded in the attempt to find universal "laws"; economic behavior is not assumed to be random, but follows predictable patterns that govern how human individuals and their societies make choices about the use of scarce resources.

For economists, scarcity has traditionally been treated as human, relative, and immediate. That is, resources are typically viewed as scarce relative to the demands for their use by existing human beings, especially those with the ability to pay. Relative scarcity means that the only concern rests with the fact that of all the resources available to satisfy certain needs, some are scarcer than others. The essence of economic analysis is to determine how best to use those relatively scarce resources. That clearly drives economists toward short-run "efficiency" in the use of resources. In fact, insofar as economists talk about the "common good" it is in the context of maximizing efficiency so that the society can exercise the greatest total amount of material consumption. And so the common good is equivalent to the interests of those with the greatest ability to produce and consume goods. Most economists do not seem to be concerned about either who does the consuming or what the impact of the production and consumption may be on nature. The approach is inevitably short-term and does not require that resource use be sustainable in the long run. One part of the economic problem has always been to find ways to substitute the relatively abundant resources for the relatively scarce ones. Market-based economic analysis argues that the price system is what ensures appropriate substitution. As a particular resource becomes scarce, its price rises and that encourages the search for alternative sources that are more abundant and therefore cheaper. In socialist systems, the same process of substitution takes place, but rather than using price changes to ensure the use of alternatives, central planning and rationing are the appropriate tools. In neither case is the care of the earth an explicit issue; in reality, each sees the common good as only the good of some particularly powerful group of *human* beings.

Market systems, using prices as the allocation mechanisms, are "efficient"; they produce greater amounts of material goods and services. One of their flaws is that the distribution of the product depends on the initial distribution of economic power in the forms of income and wealth. Those who own the most wealth will usually get the most income. That in turn will give them the greatest ability to buy and use the goods and services being produced. Thus the benefits may be distributed in ways that we consider to be unjust and to perpetuate past injustice. More to the point for this study, the pattern of resource use will then reflect the interests of the group, however large or small, that is at the top of the distribution of wealth and income. In our own society, that ownership is clearly skewed toward a relatively small group that is white and male. And their choices about resource use may well not be in the best interests of the society or the ecological system at large.

Socialist systems, using central planning and rationing as the allocation mechanisms, may be able to address the problem of injustice by imposing a different distribution mechanism. In pure socialist systems taxation coupled with transfer and spending programs by government distribute the benefits in ways that are supposed to reflect a higher level of social justice, and social welfare, than the market. One of their flaws is that they must use far more resources in the allocation activity itself and then are left with a smaller output of goods and services available for consumption.

Since most of our experience is with market systems, and since those systems seem to dominate the present order, we will couch most of the argument that follows in market terms. Under the existing market paradigm, any economic production or consumption activity, such as growth in material output, is considered to be a "good" if it enhances human well-being. In pure market economies we would try to impose Pareto optimality conditions—a proposed new activity enhances human well-being and is therefore a "good" if it makes at least one person better off without making anyone else worse off.[10]

This standard neoclassical treatment deals only with relative scarcity because it concerns itself primarily with the issue of resource allocation. That places the focus on the question of how to use the resource efficiently rather than whether to use the resource at all.[11] When neoclassical economics admits to the possibility of market inefficiency or failure, the cost of such inefficiency is almost always viewed in terms of distribution. That is, when the institutional framework seriously limits the allocative efficiency of the market, then the result is seen in the form of distributional inequity—the resulting distribution of income does not satisfy the criteria for Pareto optimality. And the solutions proposed from this traditional viewpoint involve the restoration of Pareto optimality; they suggest imposition of user fees that adjust the market or a change in the assignment of property rights. Pareto optimality does not allow for the possibility that societal welfare could be enhanced by reducing the well-being of the elite in order to improve the well-being of the underclass; and they certainly do not suggest that the "well-being" of nature ought to ever be a concern in economic decision making.

In fact, the approach ignores a third possibility, one that moves beyond allocation and distribution issues to argue that the scale of operation is too large,[12] and therefore any longer-term or perichoretic notion of the common good cannot be considered. We would add that the traditional approach is also ahistorical because it ignores the impact that human decision making in one time period has on the availability of resources in another time period. The admission of these possibilities shifts our focus from microeconomics to macroeconomics and from relative to absolute scarcity. Traditional economic thinking about the environment is micro-oriented. Allocative efficiency and distribution both attend to questions about the *individual's* use of and access to resources; that is, Is there enough of a particular resource currently available for a particular current use? Scale has a macro orientation. In the case of the environment, scale questions explore the extent of the overall level of economic activity: is the existing resource base large enough to support, on an ongoing basis, the current level of economic activity?

When the issue of scale moves to the fore, so does the question of sustainability. Now the possibility emerges that some scales of operation may be so large that they cannot be supported by the resource base. At the very least, that implies an absolute limit on the amount of economic activity that can take place during one time period—the full employment of existing resources with existing technology. Given that, it becomes appropriate to ask the question, Can the combined growth in technology and the availability of resources allow for the production of goods and services to expand without limit over time?

Traditional economic analysis has always answered this question in the affirmative: technological change and resource substitution, both generated by price changes, can, over time, keep ahead of constraints imposed by limited resources. Limited resources coupled with growing resource use will cause prices to rise. We have already suggested that rising prices are supposed to encourage substitution of the cheaper and more abundant resources. In addition, rising prices can make it profitable to invest in the creation of new technology that is either resource saving or allows for the use of more abundant resources. This can happen only if the historical pattern of resource use is appropriate. For example, we have claimed that the dominant technology for energy production in the industrial countries has centered on the burning of fossil fuels. That has in turn generated a whole series of products and consumption patterns that are energy dependent. In the United States, as we have earlier suggested, we are "locked in" to a technology that makes it extraordinarily difficult to substitute other forms of energy in the transportation sector. We have evolved a pattern of use there that is heavily dependent on petroleum and private automobiles, and that historical fact severely limits our possibilities for technological change and resource substitution.

It is our contention that traditional analysis is defective because its central theses about scarcity are flawed. First, we argue that scarcity must be addressed not just in terms of the needs of existing human beings, but also in terms of the needs of human beings into an indefinite future. That tells us that the historical past and present can affect the future. Second, we believe that scarcity must be addressed not just in terms of human need and human life, but also with respect to the place of nature in the common good. If, as Cardinal Bernardin has suggested, there is a "seamless web" of life issues,[13] then that web must encompass and be responsive to more than merely human concerns. Both of these arguments are founded on a further central proposition, which is consistent with Daly's arguments about the importance of scale: the scarcity with which economists must deal may well be absolute as well as relative.

This last proposition calls forth one of the paradigm shifts we will suggest. Both capitalist and socialist economics approach scarcity as a problem of finding the right technology, which will allow relatively abundant resources to substitute for relatively scarce ones. While we agree that that is an important constituent part of any economic analysis, we also contend that there are at least some resources for which there are no substitutes. Thus, traditional economic analysis cannot really tell us how to allocate those resources. To be sure, there are analyses that talk about the optimal rate of use of such exhaustible resources.[14] But those analyses assume that some material or technological substitute *must* exist for every exhaustible resource. When any particular resource is completely exhausted there will be a smooth transition to an alternative. The economic system will not grind to a halt.

What concerns us is the possibility that there are some resources—clean air and water, for example—that are absolutely essential to continued existence for human beings and for nature itself, and there are no viable substitutes. No matter what we may do to raise the ostensible material well-being of contemporary human actors in this case, the damage to the environment ensures that the common good will suffer. One of the uses of the air is as a dumping ground for polluting waste products. When we use the air in that way, we reduce the possibilities for using it to sustain life. Relative scarcity theories would have us continue to use the air as a dumping ground until the price of that use rose so high that we would find it attractive to use substitute dumping grounds or to recycle waste products. Socialist systems would try to arrive at the same position by substituting collective human judgment in place of the price mechanism. Both approaches miss an essential point. It is quite possible that by the time the cost of using the air rises to a high enough level to force extensive substitution the damage will have been done; the cost solutions may kick in too late. The scale of production and waste dumping may have so reduced air quality by that time that we will be on an irreversible downward spiral leading to a situation in which the air can no longer sustain human life and the richness and diversity of nature. We really don't know what will happen as a result of attempts to expand overall resource use without limit. For example, what are the consequences of that ever enlarging hole in the ozone layer and is it reversible? The point is that the assumption of absolute scarcity may place severe limits on the panacea of resource substitution.

That, of course, makes the issue of resource availability a problem of both absolute scarcity and knowledge: When will we reach the point of no return? Unfortunately, we have no way of guaranteeing that the appropriate knowledge will be acquired before we reach the crisis. Faced with that possibility, it is simply too dangerous to use the relative scarcity paradigm as the central feature of an economic system's scarcity analysis. We are moved, then, to build a new economic analysis on the foundation stone of absolute scarcity.

Now one might ask the question, Why would you call such a seemingly confining analysis of scarcity a "liberation economics"? Our answer draws on the meaning we assign to the term *liberation* and to our belief that any meaningful economic analysis must encompass the needs of nature and future generations of human beings. Liberation for us means that we are freed from restrictions imposed by the status quo and its supporting institutional arrangements. That status quo currently is structured around human domination and subordination, both in relation to other human beings and to nature. The goal of liberation is, for us, an end to domination and the ascendance of mutuality, a recognition of the reciprocal and symbiotic relationships that exist among all the parts of nature. An economics that moves us in that direction is then liberating.

The economic analysis inherent in this agenda calls for a double paradigm shift: from an anthropocentric focus to one we might call naturocentric, and from relative to absolute scarcity. As we have pointed out earlier, the purpose of economics is to allocate resources in such a way as to maximize societal welfare. The first paradigm shift requires us to establish a new definition of society for our welfare-maximizing activities; attention is given to what is good for nature. The second shift requires us to impose a new set of absolute resource constraints on those activities. Both shifts enlarge the lens in order to bring a perichoretic notion of the common good into play.

The shift to a naturocentric focus would require changes in our "rules" for making choices. We need to think about the distributional impact of our choices. But we must also remember that we are part of the natural order and thus there is an impact of our choices on nature and an impact of nature on our choices. For market economies, Pareto optimality—someone is better off without anyone else being worse off—would have to mean that both the "better off" and the "not worse off" include nature. For example, the construction of a housing development could be seen as a good only if it made human populations better off without damaging populations of other species.

Of course, under the prevailing paradigm, no real-world economic system fits the pure model. Expanding the scale of almost any human production and/or consumption activity involves the use of resources and the generation of waste products; increased welfare for some human beings is bought at the expense of the decreased welfare of some other species, and other human beings, both now and in the future. As a result of the contemporary and anthropocentric focus of modern economics, nature is very rarely accorded any status or given any value in the choice mechanism except insofar as nature can be used to serve human interests.

The second paradigm shift, from relative to absolute scarcity, highlights the weakness of the anthropocentric perspective. In the short run, where most economists focus, the idea of relative scarcity works as long as your optimality criteria include only the welfare of human beings. As economists have been claiming for two hundred years, it is quite possible that producing and consuming goods in a context of specialization and exchange can lead to a situation in which all human beings are better off today than they were yesterday. It is not a zero-sum game in which "winners" imply that there must be "losers." Price or even central planning mechanisms can shift us from relatively scarce to relatively abundant resources in ways that make all of us "winners." But even in this purely human context, absolute scarcity creates a different picture. If there are absolutely scarce resources essential to the existence of the human species, then continued use of those resources inexorably diminishes their availability to serve human needs and to sustain human life. Whatever our gains may be in terms of material goods and services, we are all "losers" if the earth runs out of clean water, clean air, or ozone.

Of course, when we impose a naturocentric focus, the problem of absolute scarcity becomes even more significant. "Losers" occur much more rapidly when we admit the possibility of any species becoming a loser when the environment necessary to sustain its existence gets used up. If, therefore, we impose naturocentrism and absolute scarcity as new controlling paradigms in the process of economic decision making, we do reduce the choices for expansion of human well-being in the world. But, at the same time, we increase the choices for expansion of the well-being of all species, including future generations of human beings.

Sustaining an ecosphere demands a complex set of interactions among plant and animal species and the geophysical environment. With that complexity comes the possibility that a seemingly minor change may begin an irreversible trend that permanently alters and perhaps destroys the ecosphere. When the scale of economic activity is constantly being expanded and is therefore pushing against the short-term resource and technology limits, the chances for beginning such an irreversible trend are large. How do we minimize that probability?

One obvious answer, and one that Daly would see as necessary, is to reduce the scale of economic activity.[15] The question is not so much whether that needs to be done, but how to do it. A paradigm shift involves a value shift, it represents a new position from which to view the world. But a paradigm shift is more than just a change to an alternative worldview. It also changes both the way we do analysis and the outcomes of that analysis. Certainly for the modern industrial countries, the growth ethic is heavily ingrained in the social ethos. Insofar as such societies concern themselves with human disadvantage, they almost universally claim that the disadvantaged's hope for betterment comes from growth. No society is going to make the move from "more is better" to "less is better" easily. In terms of the analysis itself, imposing the constraint of absolute scarcity on the system means that the traditional way of doing analysis for a market system no longer holds at every point. That traditional way has been to allow relative prices to define the degree of scarcity and then act accordingly. Our contention is that the relative price system faces the danger of pushing the use of particular resources beyond the point of no return well before price signals would make those resources too expensive to use. This means that we must make a prior decision about the scale of economic activity, including how much of that resource it is safe to use and for what purposes. Then we could add taxes or user fees to raise the price of the resource until its use is restricted to safe levels. A more extensive treatment of the impact of this approach on economic analysis will be presented in chapter 4.

Traditional resource allocation/substitution models make the assumption that there are two kinds of resources used in the production process: basic resources, or the factors of production, and intermediate resources, inputs like microchips that are manufactured by the factors of production and then used to produce other, final goods and services. Cutler Cleveland suggests an alternative way to look at resources. He essentially creates three categories:

1. Basic I—primary factors of production such as fossil fuels or the quantity of land; these are a result of natural forces and cannot be created within the socioeconomic system.
2. Basic II—other factors of production such as labor or arable land; these can be created but not manufactured by human action within the socioeconomic system.
3. Intermediate—inputs like microchips, machine tools, or gasoline; these are manufactured resources.[16]

The reason why this recategorization is important is because it separates out the resources in ways that allow us to talk about different levels of substitution. In the traditional model, the inputs are factors of production, land, labor, capital, and entrepreneurial ability. Technology tells us how to combine these factors most effectively to accomplish our production goals. Changes in relative prices of the factors of production push us to change our production technology so that we use less of the more expensive inputs and more of the cheaper inputs. The relative scarcity paradigm posits the possibility of a continuum of available or potential technologies, which will allow a virtually infinite substitution of more abundant resources in place of less abundant resources.

That possibility may be true for the Basic II and Intermediate resources that fall into categories 2 and 3 above, but not for those Basic I resources in Cleveland's first category. For example, continued growth in the material production of goods and services requires, according to the laws of thermodynamics, the use of the air or atmosphere as a sink for the deposit of waste products. At the same time, the atmosphere represents an environmental amenity necessary for the survival of the ecosphere and its rich biological diversity. At some level these two uses for the atmosphere come into conflict with one another. The nature of airsheds, like watersheds, is that they can, within limits, break down and absorb some waste products without any long-term diminution of air quality. That is, within some limits and with some waste products, the atmosphere has its own natural recycling capacity. But that capacity is limited and there is no possibility of an infinite substitution of material production and consumption, in place of biodiversity. That is, we cannot indefinitely use the atmosphere both as a sink and as a life-sustaining resource. The hole in the ozone layer, to which we have been continually referring, provides an example of the costs of assuming relative scarcity in a situation of absolute scarcity.

Human beings are not always insensitive to these issues; we *have* begun to recognize the limitations described above. But our responses continue to be couched in terms of relative scarcity and the technological feasibility of substitution. We are mired in metaphors and paradigms that turn us back to the status quo and to anthropocentrism; the common good is quite narrowly defined. When we think about air quality, we want to rely on microeconomic allocation and distribution mechanisms to solve individual problems of damage from diminished air quality, and we want to rely on technology to find ways to clean the air once it has been dirtied. We seem quite eager to ignore the macroeconomic question of the scale of economic activity and its impact on the fixed air quality resource base with which we all must live.

Our argument can be summarized as follows: We have suggested the inclusion of absolute scarcity in the economist's assumption base. We have also argued for a naturocentric as opposed to an anthropocentric worldview. The addition of the macroeconomic issue of scale to the already existing microeconomic issues of allocation and distribution begins to reshape the analysis in the appropriate direction. In addition, the recategorization of resource inputs to the production process allows us to isolate that set of resources for which absolute scarcity may be a contemporary phenomenon. Each of these changes can help to expand the notion of the common good and help the economic system serve that good more effectively.

The Godless Market and the Marketless God

In U.S. society, any consideration of the common good has to give attention to the phenomenon of the market. That attention not only involves us with economic theory, it also calls for an examination of religion in relation to the market. The church and its theologians in the United States have a long history of concern for economic justice, but they have rarely focused on "the economic system . . . as the locus for equity." Douglas Meeks notes that "North American churches seem able to wrestle on a relatively sustained basis with almost all public issues except those touching on the economy."[17] When they do respond it is usually with a mix of charity and solidarity. Food pantries, meals on wheels, shelter for the homeless, have been evidences of charity. Reinhold Niebuhr's identification with the auto workers in Detroit during the 1930s and the response to the condition of workers in the mills in Gastonia, North Carolina,[18] are examples of solidarity. However, what characterizes these moves is that they are actions "after the cards have been dealt." They are responses to the inequity that gets created when the economic system makes production and allocation decisions without regard to justice. They generally do not address the issues of power that determine who or what is controlling the "game." That is, "Who deals?" or, "What are the mechanisms by which the rules of the game are created?" Those questions generate profound implications in terms of "who pays" and how much they pay.

We agree with those who have argued that the way we think about God shapes the way we understand ourselves *and our institutions*. The issue that Meeks has enabled us to join is that of God and the market, or what does the absence of God mean for the market?[19] It does not seem unreasonable to claim that the market is "a-theistic." We might then capsulize a part of Meeks's concern with the question, "Can atheistic capitalism create a just society?" Our answer is negative. And that is not because the market and capitalism are evil in themselves but because without a God concept as a correlative reality they exclude the vulnerable, promote dominance, and idolize possessions. And, as we will consider in the next chapter, the content of the God concept also makes a significant difference.

Sallie McFague contends that there is a "demonstrable continuity"[20] in the Christian message through the ages. What distinguishes the prophetic side of faith is that it is destabilizing in challenging worldly standards, inclusive in reaching for the weak, and nonhierarchical in opposing privilege and abstraction.[21] We adjust that argument only to the point of bringing it to focus upon our understanding of God. The divine reality, therefore, calls for a message that is destabilizing, inclusive, and nonhierarchical. To talk about God in the context of the market is to claim from an institution what it does not instinctively give! If we could reverse our argument for the moment, we could say that the absence of God from the market enables it to exclude those most in need, enshrine privilege, and assign to itself the qualities of ultimacy. The presence of God in relation to the market would challenge privilege, reveal dominance, and preclude carelessness. What the reality of God does in relation to the market is make the necessary conditions for "human livelihood"[22] nonnegotiable, for those conditions are defined by the work of the divine in human history.

The ideas that underlie most market theory are profoundly individualistic. The notion of pursuing scarce resources, the security that comes from private property, and the right to consumption are all predicated on the notion that the goal of the market is to enable individuals to succeed in it. In the words of Daly and Cobb, "The world that economic theory normally pictures is one in which individuals all seek their own good and are indifferent to the success or failure of other individuals engaged in the same activity."[23] That leads to the cynical slogan, "whoever dies with the most toys wins." It is not in the nature of the market to be concerned with or create "the common good," although Adam Smith assumed that it would. Here again the dominant assumption is that we are not constituted by our relationships but are separate entities free to pursue self-interest. Human existence is solitary rather than in solidarity. At best, "the gain of the society as a whole is viewed as identical with the summation of the increase of goods and services acquired by the individual members."[24] To the degree that "G.E. brings good things to life," it is an unplanned coincidence of interests rather than a commitment to social well-being.

Nevertheless, our economic life is currently dominated by the ascendancy of capitalism. There are those who would, drawing in part on traditional individualistic theologies, ascribe the current triumph of capitalism to moral superiority. One basis for their claim is that capitalism allows "democratic" choice in the marketplace, a parallel to the political democracy that assures the rights of individuals. Of course, they fail to mention that this economic democracy is quite unevenly distributed, being available only to those who have dollar votes to exercise. We need to examine carefully their claim as well as the tension between the assumptions that support the claim and the reality of life within capitalist societies. As Weaver and Jameson argue in *Economic Development: Competing Paradigms,* every economic system attempts to promote the "good life."[25] For orthodox capitalism, the good life is always and most fundamentally defined to be increases in the material output of goods and services. That is, if the gross national product available per person is growing, then the society is doing well. The faster that measure of individual well-being grows, the better we are doing.

If we accept this as the central tenet of the good life, then there is real logic in using a market structure characterized by private ownership and control of the means of production. If more is better, then each of us should have as our prime operational goal using all of the resources we have as efficiently as we can. Economists call that achieving full employment by using all resources and full production with maximum efficiency. This would allow us to get as much output of goods and services as we possibly can. And if we devote a reasonable part of that output to the creation of increased resources via investment in new capital goods, the result will be an increased ability to produce goods in the future.

How does the capitalist market economy accomplish this magic? It requires the combination of the private ownership of the means of production and the existence of competition. If the production of goods and services is primarily accomplished by small producing units that produce output that is basically the same for all producers, then there will be lots of competition. The buyer will buy from the producer with the lowest prices. As long as consumers are free to choose what products they wish to buy and which suppliers they wish to buy them from, then producers are locked in to a situation where their own pursuit of profit forces them to act in the interest of the consumers. That drives the whole society toward the good life, increased availability of material goods and services. If a producer wants to have customers, make profit, and stay in business, there will be powerful pressure to be efficient, both to hold down costs of production and to maintain product quality. If all producers are under pressure to be efficient, we would expect the output of goods and services to be at a maximum—no wasted effort or resources. And since it is consumer choice that dictates which goods and services will be produced, we will be maximizing the output of those things that consumers want. The pressure to be efficient will also drive producers to search for new technology, a better way to produce, and that should lead to investment that will foster economic growth. Thus competition drives a capitalist system and forces it to achieve its notion of the good life over time.

Consider for a moment the polar opposite of such a system, one in which decisions about the production of goods and services are made by only one producer and where consumers of a product will have to buy the products that producer chooses to provide. Since the producer is assured of sales, there is no particular pressure to be efficient or to continually adopt new and better production technology. Therefore, the material notion of the good life will be less fulfilled than it will be under the competitive market model.

There is another supposed feature of the capitalist model that intends to further ensure efficiency. The rewards paid to the various inputs into the production process—the wages to labor, the rent for land and natural resources, etc.—are supposed to reflect the productive contributions of those resources. Thus, more efficient, more productive laborers get higher wages than less efficient ones. Once again, competition will drive all of the owners of resources to maximize the efficiency of their resource contribution because that will maximize productivity and economic reward.

So capitalism must be superior. Its institutions generate more and more of the goods and services that consumers want, and it allows consumers to share in that abundance of output on the basis of a very objective criterion, personal productivity. Clearly, God must be on the side of capitalism—it does so much good. Unfortunately, that "good" is always defined in terms of the material well-being of individual human beings; as we have argued, that is not always the same as the common good.

A Critique of Capitalism

One of the most widespread assumptions in our society is that capitalism is inevitable and the only appropriate companion of democracy. As such, it is often exempted from scrutiny. Allegiance to democracy is tantamount to allegiance to capitalism—and the flag as well. In public discourse, the fusion of the two is often portrayed as the only gateway to the good life.

There are at least three places where the capitalist model is open to serious criticism in relation to the common good. First, the material abundance view of the good life is too simplistic. Second, the fundamental importance of competition leaves the system open to question if the conditions of competition are seriously violated. Third, the assumption that personal productivity is the key force that drives the distribution process is also open to challenge.

In the first element of our critique, we argue that the good life is only good insofar as it is good for all of creation. At the very least it must include some notion of quality of life for all, not just material abundance for individual human beings. And as a part of that there should be serious attention paid to how widely the material output is shared within the society. The question of who defines the common good is a critical one. Charlie Wilson was the secretary of defense under President Eisenhower. He made famous the dictum "What's good for General Motors is good for the country"; his dictum was one focused on the material well-being of some individuals, yet we often act as though he spoke for the whole society.

The United Nations Development Project has created a human development index to allow some minimal notions of education and health care to be added to the material production of goods and services as measures of well-being, the good life, for 130 countries. To give some idea of what such an alternative measure implies, Canada ranks eleventh in the world in terms of GNP per capita, but first in terms of human development. Denmark, on the other hand, ranks seventh in GNP, but only fifteenth in human development. Denmark's income per person is about 25 percent higher than Canada's, but Canada's life expectancy and educational attainment are enough larger than Denmark's to overcome the income differential.[26] Adding even rudimentary quality of life indicators seems to change the judgment about how well a particular country is doing. The point is not who is better off, but rather that our perspective on how well any society is doing depends very much on the criteria we use to make that judgment. Thinking about the good life in terms that are broader than simply material output changes our view of the effectiveness of a particular economic system for creating that good life. And, of course, the Human Development Index does not in any way account for the ecological damage that may be done by humans' pursuit of their own individualized "good life."

Second, we question the centrality of competition in achieving the good life. It appears to us that in those countries that are theoretically dominated by a capitalist market ethic, competition is as much honored in the breach as in the reality. In the United States, for example, the Fortune 500 companies are all far too large to be "small producing units which produce output that is basically the same for all producers." Each of those corporations is so large that it plays a dominant role in the market for its products. None of them simply react to consumer demands or strive to produce the best product at the lowest possible price. Each of them is actively engaged in shaping consumer demand with vigorous advertising campaigns. They very rarely compete with each other on the basis of price and quality. Instead they rely on consumer loyalty created and sustained by large advertising budgets. Given such control over the markets in which they sell their products, these large organizations are free to pursue other goals, such as increasing their size, and gaining more and more widespread market control. We're all aware of this, since we have seen the dramatic upsurge of mergers and acquisitions in this part of the corporate world over the past fifteen years. During the 1980s, for example, an average of about twenty members of the Fortune 500 disappeared each year, swallowed up by other members of the group.

Even in terms of the material output criterion, the actions of these giant firms certainly do not move us toward a better society; and they certainly do not enhance the common good. Their goals are focused on profit, and even orthodox economic theory suggests that such powerful firms will make more profit by restricting output and raising prices. In the discussion of noncompetitive economies, we suggested that "since the producer is assured of sales, there is no particular pressure to be efficient or to continually adopt new and better production technology." It is not much different in our own real world. One of the proofs of that claim can be seen in the U.S. economy's failure to invest and generate productivity-enhancing new technology during the 1970s and 1980s. One of the reasons is that large corporations, seeking to find profit in whatever way they can, have discovered that acquisition of other corporations' assets has generated rates of return in excess of those to be earned from productivity-enhancing investment in new technology and capital. In addition, the heavy debt burden engendered by their acquisitions has left them unable to support the research and development that makes for long-term growth in material output. Not many are aware of the fact that as a percentage of GDP, U.S. investment in the "growing" 1980s was not significantly larger than it was in the "stagnant" 1970s, and thus far in the 1990s that percentage has slipped once again.[27]

Third, if personal productivity were the real key to distribution in a capitalist system, then we ought to see income distribution becoming narrower over time—the gap between the top and the bottom ought to be getting smaller. That is so because those who are at the bottom will have strong incentive to raise their personal productivity in order to get a larger share of income. The reality in the United States is that there is still a reasonably large gap between the top and bottom, and perhaps more alarming, that gap has been growing over the past twenty-five years. For example, in relation to the poverty level, the bottom 20 percent of the U.S. population was actually worse off in 1988 than in 1973. Their real family income fell by 9 percent over that time period and their tax payments increased by 16 percent. They were, in absolute terms, worse off than before. On the other hand, those in the upper 20 percent of the income distribution were easily able to overcome the stagnation of the late seventies and to take maximum advantage of the expansion of the eighties. Their real family income grew by 25 percent from 1973 to 1988, while their taxes fell by 5.5 percent. The middle 60 percent of the income distribution found their condition largely unchanged. To put all of this in a different way, in 1973, those in the top 20 percent earned, on average, about seven times as much as those in the bottom 20 percent. In 1988, the top earned almost nine times as much as the bottom.[28] Clearly, the system was not working to narrow the income distribution.

Why? One very important reason is that income is not distributed solely on the basis of personal productivity. Those who own large amounts of wealth assets such as factory buildings, stocks, and bonds will be able to claim the income that flows to the productive contribution of those assets. That would be all right if ownership of such assets were, in fact, related to personal productivity. That is, if my personal productivity allowed me to earn more income and I used that income to purchase capital assets, which then generated even more income for me, my larger rewards would still be related to my personal productivity. However, as accumulation of ownership of such assets continues over time, we begin to get large rewards being paid to people for their ownership and that ownership is not connected at all to their personal productivity. Inheritance, for example, generates income that accrues to the individual whether or not that individual is personally productive. And, of course, the concentration of such wealth among a small group tends to generate even more income for them over time. In the United States, for example, the vast bulk of such wealth is owned by the top 1 percent of the population, while 90 percent of the population owns no such wealth at all.[29]

Government policy in the 1980s exacerbated this problem and caused a long history of a slowly narrowing income distribution to be dramatically reversed. The current U.S. income distribution has a wider top-to-bottom gap than at any time since 1950. Tax policy in the early 1980s was restructured in such a way as to cut significantly the taxes paid by those at the top and to increase taxes at the bottom. The goal of the policy was to increase saving and investment at the top in order to increase the capital stock and raise productivity. That was supposed to spur economic growth and eventually make everyone better off. As our data point out, it certainly helped those at the top, but there is no sign of it trickling down to "make everyone better off."

Building a sustainable economy demands treating scarcity in a different way. We believe that it requires economic analysis to take specific account of the historical reality that scarcity has different effects on different groups of people. It also demands a consideration of the way scarcity both arises from and impacts upon the natural world. The current trend in orthodox economics is to move in the direction of increasing abstraction, relying on universal applicability of the market model to solve every problem. Unfortunately, that approach does not empower everyone in this generation, let alone future generations and nature. Without such empowerment environmental degradation will remain an intractable problem, and the common good will continue to elude us.

F·O·U·R

Redirecting the Social System

We have been exploring how a concern for community brings the issue of the common good to the table. Now we want to examine the connection between the common good and a perichoretic vision. That is not a term one would hear on the main street of our college town. Yet, once it is explained, many would agree we have it, at least in some measure. And it is profoundly germane to what many citizens are striving to institute and preserve. "Perichoresis means an 'embracing,' a feeling of solidarity with one another, a reciprocal permeation."[1] A perichoretic vision is concerned with bringing "about relational and reciprocal solidarity."[2] This argues for seeing "everything that is" as like a web; one cannot tamper with a part of it without affecting the whole. One might legitimately ask about the differences between community, the common good, and a perichoretic vision in our analysis. We have presumed to deal with each in successive chapters. But have we really? At best they are distinguishable without being separable. Perhaps we could say this: Community as opposed to individualism is a category of analysis; the promotion of community elevates the common good as a primary aspiration for society; and a common good that stresses an inclusive community marked by mutuality and reciprocity requires a perichoretic vision for its enactment. Thus, the three concepts not only overlap but lead into each other.

It is not difficult to imagine the significance of perichoretic vision in relation to preserving the environment. What is disturbing is that neither of our disciplines has a compelling history in relation to it. As we have been arguing, there is a clear deficit in both of them when it comes to the natural order. The traditional modes of analysis for economics have been blind to the interests of the earth; those modes are not organized to allow for significant value to be attached to the natural order. In most of its forms, twentieth-century theology abandoned nature in favor of grace and located God's agenda only in history; nature was only the stage on which the real drama unfolded.

74

The difference between the two disciplines lies in their capacity to do otherwise. Economics as a discipline has no transcendent principle to use as a base for judging the "rightness" of actions and decisions or to establish connections among them. What it has tended to do, as we have noted, is assume that there are some universal principles of human behavior that substitute for transcendence. In the place of "gods," therefore, economics has tended to elevate some "norm" of human action, like pursuit of self-interest. Such norms may make the analysis work for some in the world, but like many false gods, they also become idols of death for others. The neoclassical market analysis, for example, seems to promise distributive justice, based on productivity, for all. But as we have argued, the self-interest that drives the analysis often turns into greed, substituting private wants for the common good, and promoting injustice for many; it violates the web.

Theology faces a similar but opposite problem. Theology is focused on the transcendent, but often its transcendent dimensions collapse into merely human vessels. Our creation and God's are blended; the acts of humankind are equated with the acts of God. When Michael Novak argues that in the beginning God created free enterprise, we have a pristine example of that. Something brutal has happened to transcendence when Novak can refer to "the modern business corporation [as] a despised incarnation of God's presence in the world."[3] It is this concern in other theological formats that leads Alexander J. McKelway to reassert the freedom of God.[4] He contends that colleagues who work both in the process mode and in the liberation mode lose their grip on transcendence as they press toward engagement with the natural and historical orders.[5] The reality of God can appear to be identical with human values. McKelway contends it is the freedom of God that blocks this disposition toward merger. Whether or not McKelway's critique of process and liberation theologies is legitimate, the issue he raises is an important one. Theologians are always struggling to maintain the balance between affirming the transcendence of God and establishing God's immanence. Sallie McFague speaks to this when she seeks to understand "God's transcendence in an immanental way."[6] Jürgen Moltmann addresses the same problem when he writes about a "transcendent immanence."[7] To the degree that theology sustains a clear sense of transcendence, there is the prospect of correction not present in economics. Theology can free itself from investiture in false idols, and it can embrace a perichoretic vision.

It is this sense of unity that Sallie McFague represents with the image of "the world as God's Body." Everything is relational and everything is reciprocal, interconnected; nothing is outside God's body. Moltmann roots this vision in the divine life and argues that the Trinity authorizes such an inclusive sense of reality. For liberation theologians "the God of life" is the transcendent reality that links all "things." "Life" then becomes the critical principle by which all actions and responses are measured. And all dimensions of natural and historical existence are joined in resistance to death. Pablo Richard argues that "when liberation theology speaks of life, it does so in a radical manner; it speaks of an option of life for all. This includes all humanity and all of nature. Life is also understood in its concrete sense: land, work, housing, food, health, education, the environment, participation and recreation."[8] These aspects of life are not seen as a series of additive modules but as a linked set of mutually supporting systems. Where God is, there is life; where God is not, there is death. Choosing God and choosing all life systems are the same. If we are to choose life, sustainability is not an alternative; it is an imperative. The God of life is the transcendent principle that promotes perichoretic unity.

What we have been moving toward is the claim that the God imagined as "the God of life" holds the economist to the task of struggling toward a perichoretic vision. This calls for economics, in theory and in practice, to promote sustainability by inviting all living systems to the table and preserving the voice of each. Then God is understood as the God of all life and of the reciprocal relationships among all the dimensions of life. The first steps in this analysis are to push forward some new theological claims. But while theology can press such claims, it cannot orchestrate their acceptance and implementation. The economist must help the household learn how to arrange itself so that the interests of all are represented and preserved. It takes a liberation economics to implement the agenda of "the God of life." Before we explore a new economic order we need to address some theological claims in terms of what we privilege and the metaphors for God.

Privileging an Ecological Vision

It may not be appropriate to refer to liberation theology as providing values or having some key doctrines; values and doctrines tend to be abstractions from the fabric of a community's faith and a codification of experiences that may no longer be real. One cannot escape, however, the reality of recurring and foundational themes. These themes originate in historical circumstances and they continue to function within them, rather than in a theoretical realm. One of the most significant of these themes is "the preferential option for the poor." It is a phenomenon that first found expression and acclamation in the final document of the Puebla Conference and was inserted by Latin American bishops.[9] Privileging may seem to be the antithesis of a perichoretic vision. In our context, however, it is the first step in achieving it.

There is no viewing, interpreting, or understanding that does not have "privileging" as an integral component. We are never innocent bystanders reporting for the evening news. What we value drives what we choose to look at, how we interpret what we see, and where we act. When some government officials responded to the 1992 riots in Los Angeles, their privileging of order was evident and their actions were in accord with it. But some others privileged the poverty and despair of those marginalized by our society, and then the issues were shaped around a very different sense of justice. The Latin American bishops are claiming that the Christian faith requires us to privilege the poor, to do our seeing and our acting in solidarity with them. Thus "the preferential option for the poor" represents a resolve to render the Christian faith with the poor and marginalized in mind. Liberation theologians never lose sight of oppression as they act and interpret the tradition. While typical theological methods may see the concern for the poor as a by-product of faith claims, liberation theologians see the faith as a by-product of solidarity with the marginalized of our society.

There can be no doubt that the consequences of the Puebla Conference "doctrines" are both remarkable and revolutionary. When the poor are the benchmark, both society and theology begin to change. We would not want to dilute and divert that commitment and perspective. *But it is* rather anthropocentric. It concerns itself with justice in relation to humankind. The issue we want to raise is expanding the notion of "privileging" to make it more inclusive. We have argued frequently for a notion of community that includes nature and the ecosystem as full participants rather than just the setting for our concerns. That goes hand-in-hand with the recognition that exploitation of the earth arises from the same sources that have generated exploitation of human beings on the basis of race, class, and gender. In our time the natural order is clearly marginalized. The consequences of its pillage and devastation are at least as outrageous as many forms of human oppression. That treatment withholds subject status from nature. What we want to argue for is simply that an ecosystem abused by modern technology and greed can have the same specificity and privilege for a starting point as oppressed humans. Beyond that, we would contend that not only are there substantial connections between oppression in history and in nature but that the one abuse is often related to and compounds the other. In the summer of 1992 the economic condition of the poor in Haiti led to desperate violations of nature in order to generate enough food to stave off starvation. In order to survive in the present, large, economically marginalized populations, condemned to small plots of marginal land, often exploit that land with double and triple cropping and other destructive agricultural practices that severely damage its future productivity.

Perhaps what we need to do is advance the notion of privileging an ecological vision. Indeed, we might begin our viewing "through the lens of ecology."[10] The task of ecology is to give priority to relationships, organic and inorganic. Ecology focuses on symbiotic interactions among the species and organisms that make up a community and the physical environment in which they live. "Ecology reveals that organisms are not only mutually related and interdependent; they are also mutually defining."[11] Although we have used the term in a theological mode, ecologists would also embrace the notion of perichoresis. Since ecology views everything as interconnected, sustainability becomes not just a goal, but a requirement. In a way, we are arguing for viewing "everything" ecologically, including and especially the poor. Then the issue becomes, Who or what is doing the defining? And one outcome of that query is that, at present, the economic arrangements are defining the individual, the society, *and* the environment. If we embrace an "ecological vision," it inevitably will come into tension with mainstream economics and its reliance upon private property as the essential tool for the distribution of scarce resources and the definition of freedom. Both economics and private property, in their own ways, violate the primacy of relationship, connection, and sustainability that are the heart of the science of ecology.

Mainstream economics uses some of the language of reciprocity, but it is essentially a-relational; it is "based on the values of stark-individualism";[12] perichoretic unity does not fit within its vision. The world it imagines is one in which the "self-consideration" of the person plays against that of others in the aggregate and somehow produces a common good. Certainly markets involve human interaction, but the goal of that interaction is always centered on the "rational calculation of self-interest"; the basic unit is singular. The presumption is that society arises from an accumulation of individual acts or decisions. The outcome of "preferences" and "rationality" supposedly is a community whose only reality is simply the acts of persons composing it. Totally obscured is the degree to which the individuals are defined in and by the social process of economic production. The subtext is that the whole is the sum of the parts, but the parts are apparently not shaped by the whole. Since mainstream economics fails at recognizing the "co-determination" of the individual and society, it obviously also ignores nature as a component of community.

Within mainstream economics the market is presumed to be the appropriate instrument of distribution. One subtext tends to be the naive notion that the market is neutral and does not serve any agenda. Through an ecological lens, however, the market is shown not to have any sense of social connectedness and interplay with the natural order. Most particularly, the market facilitates the concentrations of power that violate the interests of community, both human and natural. Bowles and Gintis[13] call attention to Albert Hirchman's distinction between "exit" and "voice." Exit involves the power of the individual to walk away, to choose A and not B or at least to defer action in the market. But that is choosing within the context of predetermined options. That behavior is very different from "voice," which is the opportunity to go off the menu by entering into relations with others in pursuit of collectively defined goals. That more inclusive form of the "culture of democracy" is not one the market generates or supports. What is overlooked or obscured is that "goods and services are indeed allocated through market exchange, but the exchanging parties are themselves transformed or reproduced in the process."[14] Instead of individuals making transactions in the market, the market defines individuals and in the process maintains certain apparent social relations. But an ecological lens exposes this view of the market as being an anathema to community in the inclusive sense in which we are using it.

It also unmasks a prevailing sense about freedom in our society. For the most part, freedom is not viewed as a relational concept but a highly individualistic one. Mainstream economics and the market further a sense of freedom rooted in the claim, "I choose." While society may be seen as setting some restrictions, what it really values is independence and self-possessed resolve. Lappe and Callicott[15] argue that we need to let "go of a zero-sum concept of freedom," which pits the welfare of one individual against that of another. What might be seen as restrictive limits on the freedom of the individual become, when viewed through the lens of ecology, "opportunities for personal expansion and enhancement,"[16] within a context where the welfare of the community is paramount. To use a simple example, requirements for recycling materials can be either burdensome from the individual freedom perspective, or extremely satisfying from the freedom in community perspective. With an ecologically sensitive approach, the reference point is no longer just the individual but the relation with others and nature. When freedom is understood in the framework of "connectedness," responsibility emerges as a primary agenda.

What we are contending is that privileging an ecological vision will give such priority to mutuality, connectedness, and community, that mainstream economics will need to be preempted, the notion of the market as a value-free distributor will have to be abandoned, and freedom will have to be reconceived. It will no longer be possible to define the common good as just the sum of individual human wants. But even with the change in vision it is important to remember that "who does the defining" will shape the result. That returns us to the transcendent and raises the question of God, at least for the theologian.

Old and New Metaphors for God

There likely are a number of points at which a liberation theologian might enter the environmental arena and begin to address the willful silence that has characterized most theology. The entry point that seems most promising is an examination of our claims about God and the language that we use to make them. Privileging an ecological vision pushes us to explore more completely existing and alternative metaphors for God, and to consider whether or not they contribute to perichoretic unity.

That there should be a critique of God concepts in response to pressing contemporary issues is not a unique contribution of liberation theology. Critique of our language for God is central to the theological enterprise. What liberation theologians have inserted is the sense that the location from which that critique occurs and who formulates it are first-order considerations. Where the language gets formulated is integral to a responsible articulation; who does the asking shapes the image and metaphors that are finally advanced. Meeks's approach has been of particular interest to us. He raises the question of God in an economic framework, seeking a metaphor for God that will connect with political economy. When the true "God does not appear in the modern market,"[17] then this absence leaves the welfare of human beings out of the story.

That is, the language of the market is entirely individual and human-centered; there is a "faith claim," but it has nothing to do with a transcendent God. Because of this language deficit, neither the church nor theology is able to influence the economic order. Meeks then proceeds to advance the image of "economist" as a consequential way of representing the reality and activity of God, thus opening up the economic order to theological claims.

We are suggesting that the paralysis of theology in relation to valuing nature and including it within the perimeter of community bears a similar relation to God concepts. One can divert a claim by Anna Case-Winters from "the realm of human affairs" and transpose it as follows: "The way in which we conceive of God and the way we speak of God have real consequences . . . [for the environment]. The theological constructs we employ may be said not only to reflect and express values we already hold, but also to inform and determine our valuations."[18] We need to remind ourselves that our language for God is not just an inert label, a means of referencing. Our imagery is defining not only of the nature of divine activity but also our posture in relation to it. The naming of God and the naming of a child are not the same act. There are consequences and implications for "what are you going to call God?" that are not present in "what are you going to call your baby?" The name I give my child says little about who I am or my relationship to the infant. When I use metaphor to name the ultimate, I am not only attempting to recognize what God is about but also to describe my own responsibilities.

For example, it does not take much imagination to see how images of God as King and as Omnipotent authorize dominance and control as appropriate forms of human agency in nature and elsewhere. God as King rules and reigns in ways that restrict both freedom and responsibilities. The omnipotent One takes care of things and the individual is reduced to a docile servant. The life-giving and life-affirming dimensions of God's power are eclipsed. It is easy to lose track of the reality that such metaphors, our God concepts, arise out of circumstances and in historical settings; they carry with them the values prevalent there and in time have consequences in settings for which they were not conceived. God as King was derived in another era with different concerns; it does not, in our time, inspire perichoresis or invite us to assume responsibility for the earth; it is the antithesis of connectedness.

When we use the liberation mode and emphasize location and voice, the transition to environmental issues is neither smooth nor swift. Liberation theology calls for conscientization of the oppressed; nature does not lend itself to "conscientization" and the call for a voice seems strained to our anthro-centered ears. At one level, of course, nature does "talk back"; it reacts to mistreatment in the form of unusable environments. But reaction does not attribute intrinsic value to nature. The usual "voice" in liberation theology is the authentic cry of the oppressed; it may be reactive in part, but it is also creative, pushing toward the enactment of a new community "from the bottom up." The phenomenon of the trashing of nature can help, however, as we search for a location for our critique of God concepts. What image of God can function to make nature important enough to change our behavior and lead us to be proactive in the midst of the impact of the burning of fossil fuels on global warming, the consequences of erosion and overcultivation on food supply, and the effects of deforestation on biodiversity? We need to identify a God concept for nature that furthers perichoresis and accomplishes for the environment what "God the Economist" does for the market.

There are some significant examples of this process. The way in which Sallie McFague reworks the trinity from Father, Son, and Holy Spirit to Mother, Lover, and Friend is both imaginative and persuasive.[19] She restores intimacy and relevance to the connection of God and creation. McDaniel's reference to God as "cosmic Heart" suggests ways of healing our tortured relationship to the earth. That relocates God at the center of all earthly processes. Both theologians evoke and represent a "new sensibility," which focuses on interrelationship and interconnection in order to override the individualistic and autistic tendencies of our age. It is tempting to seek a way of grafting their metaphors and analyses onto our agenda. But their efforts ride on a process theology model that is not our own. Because we approach the issues, at least initially, from the historical perspective of liberation theology, the metaphors we seek need to be congruent with that different theological method and tradition.

For liberation theology, Gustavo Gutiérrez is a "church parent." His work may not have been seminal for black and feminist theologians in the United States, but in a global framework he has to be acknowledged as "first among equals." At the level of theological method few have escaped his influence. In a recent publication he focuses on "the God of life," which is both his God concept and the title of the book.[20] We want to explore that image to see if it addresses the location from which we are seeking a new metaphor.

In his first work Gutiérrez argues that "human history . . . is the location of our encounter with him, in Christ."[21] The preeminent biblical promise is the presence of God to God's people and humankind is called to acts of justice on behalf of the poor and oppressed.[22] God "deals out justice to the oppressed. The Lord feeds the hungry and sets the prisoner free,"[23] calling us to "a conversion to the neighbor, the oppressed person, the exploited social class, the despised race, the dominated country."[24] The location of theology must be congruent with God's reality and work. The theological representation that follows from this is, for Gutiérrez, fully articulated later as "the God of life." The issues for the poor and oppressed are life and death, and God is in one and against the other. To be more specific, the hunger for God and the hunger for bread may not be the same but they cannot be separated. "Faith in God must lead to elimination of the lack of bread."[25] Because God is the God of life and not death, "faith and starvation cannot be combined."[26] Bread and God are not interchangeable but in the midst of starvation they are one. God is on the side of life and whenever one chooses life one chooses God.[27] The fullest expression of this is the resurrection, when life overrides death, the oppressed are liberated from the oppressors, and the final word is always "the God of life." Initially it would seem that this God concept is exclusively linked to the historical process and is of little value in relation to the natural order.

Without in any way diminishing or diluting the presence and activity of God in the historical realm, Gutiérrez attempts to extend the presence of God to the cosmos. "God is present in everything that is a result of God's creative action."[28] As a consequence of that there are "traces of God in the natural world."[29] That is an acknowledgment that does not usually accompany the identification of God in the historical process of liberation. Not wanting in any way to limit the presence of God, Gutiérrez claims that "God is manifested on the mountain and in the storm, and in the fire amid thunder and lightning. . . . God is also manifested in the 'tiny whispering sound' of a breeze, in the light caress that restores calm after the terrifying storm."[30]

We would be imperialistic as "first world" academics to tell Gutiérrez where to encounter God. For the poor and oppressed the God of life has to be the One who comes down on the side of their historical struggle for freedom and is manifest in their community. Our concern is more explicitly with a move that "nudges" God over into the realm of nature with a version of the claim that there is nowhere where God is not. We contend that Gutiérrez is making a claim that is more promising for nature when he says, "When I speak of life, I mean all life."[31] God's covenant is with "all that is" and the whole of creation awaits liberation, the end of oppression, the triumph of life over death. What we specifically want to claim is that in the location of environmental deterioration, the metaphor of God as "the God of life" has more promise than the rationale Gutiérrez offers. Gutiérrez provides this panentheistic version of his metaphor only as a kind of "add-on" to the God that is found in history. We argue that nature is more integral than that. In a profound sense nature and history are drawn together in the reality of the poor. If we take seriously our earlier contention that the human economic system is embedded in a wider ecological system, then "the God of life" must be saying more than "give my people bread." We need an understanding of God that moves in the direction of an "empowering spirit" who works for "the healing and wholeness of community" and summons us "to act in harmony with God."[32]

Indeed, the existing economic system can and does create the needed bread. Unfortunately, it often does that in a way that so damages the natural order that some nonhuman parts of nature cannot be sustained. The "hamburgerization" of some of the Latin American rain forest is a case in point.[33] The rain forest is being stripped away to provide grazing land for raising beef cattle that will ultimately supply the fast-food restaurants of the world. In the process, species are irrevocably lost and the biosphere becomes less capable of sustaining the complex web of life. And, of course, even in the purely human sphere, any such damage to the natural order may also make sustaining the creation of bread for the long run problematic. "The God of life" then seems to be saying that "starvation" is a phenomenon that ultimately affects all life and therefore imposes a responsibility for all life. Life over death means liberation both from historical oppression and the devastation of the environment, which is integrally linked to it. "The God of life" can clearly create hope both for marginalized human beings and for a marginalized environment in all its convulsions.

Sallie McFague has encouraged us to think of theology as "a heuristic venture," one that tries out new metaphors for God without embarrassment or overconfidence.[34] In that spirit, we want to offer an image for God that might, along with others, give new texture to the linkage between God, the natural order, and ourselves. We want to imagine that "the God of life" is *gentle*. That word may take us in some directions that would not be productive. "Gentle" can imply some of the nuances of "ineffective." "He is too gentle to function in a corporate setting" might be an example of that. The term can suggest too little backbone or spine, a core that cannot cope with reality as it is configured daily. The harsh side of the judgment is that "gentle" participates in fundamental weaknesses. But strength and gentleness need not be terms at odds with each other; neither are liberation and gentleness in tension. Those who have experienced the rhetoric of Alcoholics Anonymous know that "tough love" is not a contradiction in terms. Indeed, we could argue that only the gentle are really strong. An ear and nose surgeon we know has fingers and hands that appear to have been fashioned for pounding on an anvil and disciplining steel to forms it would resist. But to the touch he is gentle and what appear to be stubs can work instruments in intricate procedures. Seeing ourselves in the image of a gentle God rather than an omnipotent one could change our relationship to nature. It could lead us to value nature for itself and include it in our sense of community.

"Gentle" assures that the God of life cannot be construed to be regal rather than relational; it protects the connective and persuasive activity of God from being understood as coercive. The image of the gentle God of life affirms that everything is subject and nothing is object to God. And this image acts on us in ways that transform our relationships in the community of "all that is." When we acknowledge that God is on the side of nature and against its exploiters, that God is as fully present in the natural order as in the historical one, that God influences the direction and destiny of the natural order, then this authorizes and evokes in us a different relationship to nature. We become relatives, indeed blood relatives. We may not think, with Alice Walker's Shug, that cutting a tree will make our arm bleed, but a kinship has been established whose bonds and ties are inexhaustible. Then we can begin to allow nature to be all that it is and we are liberated from a consumer-induced need to violate it. The gentle God of life empowers us to live lightly on the earth rather than abusively, to join the perichoretic unity that God embodies and intends.

Unfortunately, the image of "gentle" also works in several directions, and the consequences for our relationship with nature are not all positive. The term "gentleman" makes that evident. In its origin, the term is inherently hierarchical and creates the very dualisms that must be avoided. A gentleman is one who is well-bred, privileged by birth; the term strokes social position. Civility is paramount, but without any necessary tempering by morality or justice. "Gentleman" is, then, a term for thinly veiled dominance, and to use "gentle" for God could impose the very patriarchal qualities we seek to avoid. But the dark side of the image need not prevail. "Gentle" also works in the direction of compassion, mildness, patience, and meekness. Its opposites include violence, tempestuousness, severity, and harshness. To be gentle is to be responsive, tender, and open to all that is "not self." It is to be inclusive, relational, and empathetic.

When we want to think about the impact of seeing God as gentle it may be particularly helpful to pick up on the synonym *meek*. That word steps forward because of its biblical usage. Two texts, which are related, come to the fore. When the psalmist (37:11) affirms that "the meek shall possess the land," the reference is to the promised land. When Matthew (5:5) records Jesus as saying, "Blessed are the meek, for they shall inherit the earth," the reference is figurative. But in both instances, where one is centered is what is at issue in extolling meekness. The meek are not centered in self; they are not involved in destructive competition in which the land is implicated; they are free of the need to be strong in the sense of power over anything other. Hence, those who are to possess the land or inherit the earth do not thrive on ownership or perceive it as a means of gaining advantage over others. They are anchored in relationship, and the defining one is with God.

Our claim has been that we should be thinking about God as "the God of life" and that the image of "gentle" suggests some of the meaning in that notion. Viewed from the human side, the quality of meekness follows from understanding God as gentle. Those who are to inherit the earth or possess the land biblically are those whose center is "the God of life"; they will "treat the earth as our kin or neighbor."[35] It does not take any substantial imagination to see that the ecological crisis is not something that originated in nature. The violation of the systems of the natural order rests solely on human initiative. It comes from the failure or unwillingness to recognize the essential connections between the humanly created economic system and a broader, nature-encompassing ecological system. It is the human drive to be dominant and the corresponding refusal to be meek that creates the death potential in the environment. The human tendency is to be hierarchical rather than perichoretic; reinforced by many theological images, humans have tried to exercise power over nature rather than mutuality and solidarity with it. Humans make the earth lethal; they violate the web; they deny the common good. And their behavior is singularly located in a self, corporate and individual, that centers on itself and its own interests. The absence of meekness gets institutionalized in worldly orders, not the least "effective" of which is economic. This is why liberation theologians have contrasted "the God of life" and the idols of death rather consistently in terms of what the economy can do to our historical existence. We suggest that works as well for the economic institutions of our global environment. All the traditional models focus on human satiation at some tolerable or excessive level. The earth exists for us and we are free to use it toward our purposes. Nature is not free to be all that it is because it is not included in community and valued for itself. The issue we want to pose is: What kind of an economic order would be consistent with "the God of life" and the elevation of the human quality of meekness?

It is at this point that economics and theology can interact. When a theologian develops or expresses a new metaphor for God, there are consequences. Certainly, as a result of the work of liberation theologians, the metaphor of "the liberating God" builds a different set of relationships, both with God and among human beings, from "the omnipotent God." Earlier, we have suggested that Meeks's "God the economist" is a metaphor that can enact a different set of relationships between God and humans and thus generate a different focus for theology and a different agenda for the society. And that focus for theology is further altered when the controlling metaphors include "the God of life" and the "gentle God." By analogy, when economists begin to assume a constraint of absolute scarcity, they are forced to build a kind of economic analysis different from that based on relative scarcity. At the very least absolute scarcity suggests that communal concerns about resource use share equal footing with individual ones, because use by anyone affects everyone.

The new metaphors for God lead to new relationships among humans and between humans and the natural order, ones grounded in perichoresis. Those new relationships have consequences for the economic realm. And absolute scarcity demands a different analysis and a new set of economic relationships in terms of the impact of human economic activity on the natural order. It is inevitable that any such new relationships with the natural order will also engender new relationships with the ultimate. And so, even as a new understanding of history and nature engendered by science and social science, especially economics, calls for a new theology, there is a mutual demand by theology for a new economics; the new economics and the new theology can only emerge from a mutual interaction.

A New Economic Order

We have argued that it is necessary to develop some alternative paradigms for economics in order to allow the discipline adequately to address environmental degradation. In particular, we have suggested that the controlling paradigms for economics must shift from anthropocentric to naturocentric and from relative scarcity to absolute scarcity. A growing body of economists, calling themselves "ecological" economists, have begun to develop an analysis that implements such a paradigmatic shift. To connect with our rhetoric, we would identify an ecological economist as one who sees the common good with a perichoretic vision and through an ecological lens.

There are two principal thrusts within this new sub-discipline. The first is the emphasis on sustainability. The second is the drive to create a steady state. The general definition of ecological economics is summarized by Costanza, Daly, and Bartholomew:

> Increasing awareness that our global ecological life support system is endangered is forcing us to realize that decisions made on the basis of local, narrow, short-term criteria can produce disastrous results globally and in the long run. We are also beginning to realize that traditional economic and ecological models and concepts fall short in their ability to deal with global ecological problems.
>
> *Ecological economics* is a new *transdisciplinary* field of study that addresses the relationships between ecosystems and economic systems in the broadest sense. These relationships are central to many of humanity's current problems and to building a sustainable future but are not well covered by any existing scientific discipline.[36]

They further argue that integration and synthesization are the critical features of ecological economics, for "while the intellectual tools we use . . . are important, they are secondary to the goal of solving the critical problems of managing our use of the planet."[37]

From the perspective of this study, one of the most crucial differences between conventional economics and ecological economics concerns the role of human beings. In conventional economics, human beings are the center of analysis, they are the actors who move things, and they move them for their own individual purposes. Humans also play a central role in the analysis of ecological economics, but here they must understand their role as being only part of a larger system, and they must be responsible for managing that system sustainably, in a way that is supportive of the symbiotic and reciprocal relationships that characterize all of nature. In addition, conventional economics believes unequivocally in the efficacy of technical progress as a tool to alleviate any relative scarcity in the resource base. Ecological economics recognizes that whatever may happen in the evolution of technology and human culture, there will continue to be significant ecological constraints on economic activity.

For conventional economics, growth models almost always prevail over no-growth models. That is because the boundary conditions that control and limit the action of the economic system are always seen as encompassing only relative scarcity. As we have claimed earlier, that means that substitution can solve any scarcity problem by finding the means to substitute relatively abundant resources for relatively scarce ones. Environmental and resource economists have really extended the same argument to the problem of negative externalities like pollution. That is, externalities also arise because of scarcity or some aspect of scarcity. If the externality problem is nuclear waste or acid rain, we will find some technological fix, which allows for an appropriate substitution that eliminates the externality. Or if the problem is scarcity of some resources such as water and air that have historically been treated as common property, then assignment of property rights will once again assure appropriate substitution.

In effect, conventional economic approaches begin with the assumption that all want-fulfillment can take place in a market context and, therefore, we can continue without limit in trying to fulfill the unlimited wants of human actors. Since those wants are unlimited, we can never fulfill all of them, but the market will allocate and it will allow us to produce more goods and services every year and thus allow more wants to be fulfilled. At any given time, the limits placed on the degree of fulfillment are set by available and usable resources and by technology. And, as we have said, those limits are only relative and capable of amelioration through time via substitution and technological change.

Ecological economics says we must begin with the laws of thermodynamics—especially the entropy law, which claims that energy and matter are constantly in a process of movement from low entropy to high entropy. This means that resources are being converted from organized and useable forms to disorganized and unusable forms. In terms of our argument, economic activity that generates increasing amounts of goods and services to fulfill human wants must at the same time be generating increasing levels of entropy. That ultimately renders the resource base unusable for further production; that is, the possibilities for growth are not infinite.

Faced with that reality, ecological economists contend that economic activity must be built on sustainability. That means that resource use must be confined to levels that can be maintained for the indefinite future. Substitution and technological change can reduce the rate at which resources in general must be used, but they cannot reduce that rate of use to zero. In our earlier discussion, we drew on the work of Herman Daly to outline the institutional framework necessary to achieve that sustainable rate of economic activity. That particular variant on the sustainability theme leads to the no-growth steady state.

One of the ways to get a handle on this approach to analysis is to think in terms of any process of producing goods and services as generating waste products, what ecological economists refer to as throughput. The entropy law states that this throughput will have a higher level of entropy than the resources initially used to create the products. Whatever our capabilities for recycling and reuse, some part of the initial energy/matter mix must inevitably become lost, unusable, as a result of the production activity. If the initial resources used are not renewable then, ceteris paribus, the capability for future production has been diminished. As long as the range of potentially available resources is large relative to current production, and as long as technology improves the choices and efficiency of our use, then conventional economics is correct and substitution allows for unlimited growth.

Ecological economists, however, dispute both the range of resource availability and the efficacy of technology. Looking at the world through an ecological lens, they posit a complex interactive set of relationships within the biosphere, wherein some extensive but unidentified level of biodiversity is necessary for the survival of all life. If the scale of human economic activity generates enough throughput to overtax the absorptive capacity of the biosphere, then the battle to use that biosphere will inevitably squeeze out some species, reducing the biodiversity. And the species that get squeezed will be those least able to defend themselves. Since we don't know where the biodiversity "cutoff point" is, we don't know how much throughput damage the biosphere can handle.

One critique of this position argues that the battle to use the biosphere is simply part of the normal evolutionary process and that the result will be one more step in the "survival of the fittest." We find that argument unconvincing for two reasons: first, human economic action is compressing the battle into far too short a time period for evolution to create effective responses; second, our anthropocentric defense mechanisms ought to push us in the direction of sustaining human life on the planet for as long as possible. The dramatic reduction in biodiversity over the last century would seem more likely to threaten rather than sustain long-term human life.

While the underlying assumptions used by ecological economists are significantly different from those of orthodox theory, when they turn to implementation of the program, they argue for modification, not abandonment, of the market system. They view that system as exceptionally good at allocating scarce resources in an efficient manner. What the market is not good at is Daly's scale problem, deciding how many resources there are to be allocated, at least not in those circumstances where the resources are common property, as is the case with most "environmental" resources like air, water, and esthetics. For example, carbon dioxide is a by-product of many natural and human-economic production processes. The biosphere has the ability to absorb and recycle CO_2, converting it into oxygen, water vapor, and biomass through photosynthesis. Human-economic production processes can overload and/or alter the absorptive/recycling capacity of the biosphere. And rapid deforestation reduces the overall capacity to reuse the CO_2 that is released into the atmosphere.

Ecological economists are convinced that conventional economic analysis is not built on an appropriate set of institutions and, as a result, does not adequately account for these excessive uses of the biosphere. Conventional analysis relies on price signals to encourage substitution. But common property resources are not "priced" in any direct sense, and even if they were, how could nature, the poor, the disadvantaged get the wherewithal to pay the price? Thus, as we argued earlier, the signals are muted, lagged, and unrepresentative. When the system finally hears the signals, the conditions of overload have typically already been in place for quite some time. Thus, even if we assumed that we human "managers" of the system had the best motives in the world, the nature of the existing arrangements is such that cycles of biosphere damage are inevitable. And since we don't know how much damage is too much, the threat of ultimate collapse is always there.

The problem can be illustrated graphically. In figure 4.1, the quantity is the available CO_2-absorptive capacity of the biosphere. D1 and D2 represent demands to use that capacity. MPC is the cost per unit that must be paid by private users to use the capacity. For example, a private business that burns fossil fuel for energy would have to build and maintain a smokestack in order to vent its CO_2 emissions into the atmosphere. Theoretically, then, it could vent large quantities of gas at a constant price per unit vented. So the MPC is drawn as a horizontal line. As the demand for its product increased, its demand to use the biosphere's absorptive capacity would increase, shifting from D1 to D2. If only the private costs are accounted for, the society would move from point A to point B, and the quantity of CO_2 dumped would rise from Q1 to Q2.

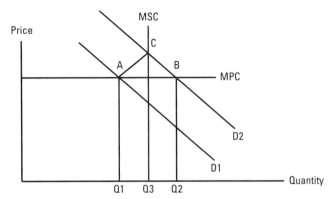

Figure 4.1

However, as the business begins to use up the scarce absorptive capacity, an externality is generated in the form of diminished air quality for the society. The cost imposed on the society by this externality is reflected in the MSC curve. If all of the costs of this production process, including the externalities, were taken into account, then the society would settle at point C, and the amount of CO_2 vented would never exceed Q3. The verticality of the MSC at Q3 indicates that the damage from additional CO_2 beyond this point is so excessive that no payment could compensate for it.

Conventional analysts believe that they account for this problem by suggesting that the excessive use at Q2 will eventually generate public dissatisfaction, which will force some control mechanisms. The Environmental Protection Agency represents just such a public response. With luck and good negotiation, the level of emissions will eventually be reduced to Q3, which is the maximum sustainable amount. Ecological economists are concerned about the impact of the "bulge" to Q2 because they are not convinced that any damage caused by exceeding the absorptive capacity is reversible.

If we want to move away from the potential trap created by conventional analysis, we need to create a new set of boundary conditions within which the market operates. If we can imagine and then implement such a new set of conditions, then we could have both the allocative efficiency provided by the market and the pursuit of communal well-being envisioned by ecological economists. Recall the alternative institutional structures that we introduced in chapter 2. One of those structures involved resource depletion quotas. What if we added those into the mix for our CO_2 problem?

One logical constraint would involve a communal decision about the appropriate quota for CO_2 emissions. That is, a level that fits inside the biosphere's recycling capability. Potential emitters would then have to bid for quota rights in an auction. Those who bought the rights would be allowed to emit CO_2, while others would not. If the penalties for violation were severe enough, emissions would indeed be limited to at or below the recycling/absorptive capacity. In terms of our graph, we would have enforced an emission cost of MSC, holding the total emissions at or below Q3. But, in this case, we do not have the "bulge" in emissions up to Q2, and hence we do not face the possibility of irreversible damage.

The most important feature of this example is that without the institutional arrangements that lead to the communal decision about the appropriate emission level, and without the creation of the quota auction, the lags in the market's response mechanisms do not allow us to get to Q3 without going through the "bulge." The proponents of the market are right; the market can be very effective at allocating resources as long as we remove the impediments, such as monopoly power, that drive a wedge between the market and social welfare. But the market still cannot accomplish the desired goal unless there is a change in the framework and setting within which market allocation takes place. In our contemporary world the framework and setting is not seen through an ecological lens and thus honors the individual self-interest of the human, contemporary, and most powerful of the society. We need to shift our priorities and find a way to honor the interests of a more inclusive community. That is, our disciplines, our society, and our lives need to embrace a sense of community driven by a commitment to the common good and shaped by a perichoretic vision.

F·I·V·E

Prelude to a New Order

One of the earliest preachers in Granville, Ohio, the Reverend Jacob Little, liked to recall that "their [the first settlers] first house of worship was built by God himself, as high as the noonday sun and as wide as the Eastern horizon is from the Western."[1] That first sabbath in the new village drew "93 precious souls"[2] around "the great red beech tree felled on the day of their arrival."[3] Nature, history, and God were joined for them on that memorable first sabbath. Somehow "souls" and "stumps" and the Divine existed in some kind of unfathomable unity. In the simplest and most profound sense, it was perichoretic, perhaps because there were not yet any institutions or local ideologies to corrupt it.

One would not find that integration now, nor a consciousness of nature as a gift from God, in our village churches. There is very little recognition of the human cost of development, and virtually none of its environmental cost; the churches' sermons, liturgies, and bulletin boards are clearly in a different place. The churches may be physically located at the center of the village, but they seem almost unaware of the degradation of nature that is taking place around them. They have neither the will, the language, nor the impulse to connect the "Lord of Creation" to the uncreation occurring in the community. One would think that religion and the environment don't mix. It need not be that way, and it is not always so at higher church levels, where "the integrity of creation" is a prominent theme. Historically, religion has almost always had a role in establishing a new order, and we want to reclaim that in relation to environmental issues.

At its best, the Judeo-Christian tradition has a "language of the heart" with which to resist the injustices and institutionalized evils of U.S. society. Over time it has been at the center of establishing new social realities. Privileging an ecological vision assumes a call to such a new reality. And so we want to consider the Jesus event as being more than a personal and historical one. If the incarnation is taken with radical seriousness it can be inclusive of the natural order. Jesus embodies, as we have argued, an ecological vision, and the event is concerned with "rightful relations" in the most comprehensive sense. Jesus embraced all creation. Yet the ecological vision, the role of religion, and the sense of radical incarnation cannot, by themselves, accomplish a change in society; that requires a transformation of the economic and social order.

From an operational point of view that means the society will value and the institutions must uphold certain tenets. In the next chapter we will identify these as an "ecological trinity":

1. The welfare of our *nonanthropocentric* community is at the center of our activity.
2. The members of the community can fulfill their interests by *mutual* action.
3. The interests of the members *connect* and interact with each other.

To do all that, new kinds of structural relationships must be established that ensure the emergence of those values and enhance the achievement of those goals.

Pervasive Inertia and the Role of Religion

One of the ironies of the 1990s is that environmental awareness and environmental deterioration are simultaneously on the rise. That certainly is counterintuitive. One would expect that two decades of scholarly exploration, media hype, and political posturing as well as the election of an environmentalist as vice president would lead to a visible challenge to the downward spiral. The presumption that "knowledge saves" has seldom been more clearly refuted. The ecocrisis grows more intense even as our understanding of it becomes more convincing. Even rational self-interest cannot seem to prevail over the threat of "uncreation." What blocks our ability to grasp "the fate of the earth" in ways that would translate into an agenda of sustainability? What blinds us to an ecological vision that would consider the future of other species and of the earth itself? Our first impulse may be to appoint villains and engage in self-serving differentiations between particular corporations and *we* environmentalists. But that is to focus on symptoms and ignore a more pervasive reality in which we all are immersed.

We have suggested what happens when individualism is coupled with an institutional system that concentrates power; the good of some overrides the common good. We can talk about a notion of community that includes nature and aspire to a recognition of interdependence, but if we continue to participate in a "dominant consciousness"[4] that renders holy individual rights and preferences, the threat of the ecocrisis will seem muted and finally echo only in the empty corridors of betrayed dreams. Or, perhaps even worse, those with wealth and power will hold the crisis at arm's length by instituting more environmental racism and imposing the damage on the poor and minorities. We are all part of what Robert Bellah calls a "culture,"[5] Max Oelschlaeger calls a "dominant social matrix,"[6] and we call an "ideology"[7] that has as its most uncontested creed the conviction that the self and its aspirations ought to be central and should be restrained only at the margins. Bellah is careful to make differentiations within the notion of individualism and he identifies its utilitarian form as the most virulent and antithetical to community. The rigorous pursuit of one's own interest, the ability of persons to secure their own advancement by their own initiative, is the social context generated by our society. "Utilitarian individualism views society as arising from a contract that individuals enter into only in order to advance their own self-interest."[8] That may sound more malignant than many in our society would want to admit, but there are subtler versions of it we might recognize: "What is great about America is that anyone can get ahead." "God helps those who help themselves." "The cream always rises to the top." "The government has become our enemy." What is absent and indeed precluded in each of these maxims is communal values. Adam Smith, the father of modern economics, is often quoted in support of this individualism: "By pursuing his own interest he frequently promotes that of the society more effectually than when he really intends to promote it."[9] Following this lead, the common good is presumed to be a consequence of self-advancement rather than a necessary condition of justice in a social order. Restated in environmental terms, the self-interest inherent in our cultural context recognizes no restraint on consumption, no claims for future generations, no place for nature beyond its instrumental value, no concern for other species, and no responsibility for nonrenewable resources. The question of sustainability cannot even get on the table. And the prospects of a perichoretic vision coming into play are forfeited.

A subtext of our contention is that language is integral to our social reality. Whether we think of it in terms of "culture," "dominant social matrix," or "ideology," our sense of reality arises by linguistic means. Symbols, metaphors, and myths originate and sustain "our sense of the way things are." And whatever or whoever controls these, shapes reality. Douglas Meeks advances an argument we want to acknowledge but utilize in a different way. He notices that "the semantic fields of economy and biblical rendering of God are surprisingly similar."[10] Meeks is certainly accurate when he calls upon us to think of terms like *fidelity, fiduciary, debt, redemption,* and *saving* as common to the two spheres; he tries to develop that common language as a source for connection. We want to contend, however, that the economic meaning of the terms has eclipsed the theological in our linguistic landscape.

The economist is one of those who create the social reality of utilitarian individualism. Financiers and economists have now become the high priests; our priorities are set by them and our institutions shaped by them. Oelschlaeger contends that the modern paradigm "articulates itself through utilitarian individualism—the language of *Homo economicus:* our first language, institutionalized through our political economy."[11] The economy not only depends on individuals seeking their own advantage, but equates moral progress with the growth that follows. It's no coincidence that in the 1992 presidential campaign one advisor had on his desk the slogan, "It's the economy, stupid." While seemingly condemning a decade of greed, the promise of a new administration was fundamentally focused on economic growth. Now what is inevitably missing in the self-centered individualistic rhetoric of growth is any sense of the well-being of the other and of the web of which we are all a part. Any impulses toward perichoresis, an ecological vision, or sustainability are stillborn. New political power coalitions can condemn or support "trickle-down theories" without ever really addressing the conditions of those at the margins, those most in need. Our secular narrative is one that equates the good life for each and the common good for all with more GNP. Quality and quantity, for some, get blended. The sources of our assurance that things are getting better are the Federal Reserve System, the Council of Economic Advisors, and the Office of Management and Budget.[12] The election of President Clinton was in large measure a result of his appeal to individual interests, carefully politicized, set to deliver through growth. The slogan now seems to be "we have to grow the economy to save the society."

The reason for our apparent digression into utilitarian individualism and its expression through the economy is to note what is missing. The environment is not a player. Building a sustainable economy and ecology is not part of the vocabulary. Nature has no voice in the conspiracy between the politics of individual interests and the economics of growth and consumption. At this point it is somewhat difficult to imagine an advisor to a president urging the use of the slogan, "It's the environment, stupid." Our culture, social matrix, and ideology have been shaped by the interests of the economy and those who benefit from its growth. In our recent history this has been one of the reasons for the privatization of religion. Faced with a public sphere dominated by "it's the economy, stupid," religion has tended to retreat to a concern for private salvation. In a sense the society is served by two high priests: Alan Greenspan tells us how we are doing with regard to personal consumption; Billy Graham tells us about our relation to personal salvation. In the situation at its worst, consumption becomes salvation in the final act of linguistic imperialism.

The question then becomes, Who can give us a new language that can create a new culture, social matrix, and ideology with nature's intrinsic worth assured? Who can define the common good perichoretically? Where will we find the myths, metaphors, and symbols along with institutional structures for a society in which utilitarian individualism is challenged and interdependency celebrated? What might trigger a decisive paradigm shift from private values that marginalize nature to communal values that marginalize self-interest and greed?

One approach would be to reverse the privatization of religion that has occurred in our society. Max Oelschlaeger argues that "there are no solutions for the systemic causes of ecocrisis, at least in democratic societies, apart from religious narrative."[13] If religion were more innocent in relation to environmental issues, that might be a more comfortable theme to entertain. While some will argue that organized religion has contributed to our crisis, others simply note its silences. At the very least it has frequently been in collusion with an economic order that facilitates utilitarian individualism. But the failures and defaults of religion ought not to distract us from its legitimating and delegitimating power. The ordering of our everyday experiences and the interpretation of their meaning achieves the status of "reality" when religion overwhelms our insecurity and its sense of precariousness and locates the experiences and their meaning in a "sacred order."[14] Berger goes on to say that "religion legitimates so effectively because it connects the precarious reality construction of empirical societies with ultimate reality,"[15] and in the process our social institutions and the values they sustain achieve "ultimately valid ontological status."[16] The world we live in is of linguistic origin and what authorizes its permanence is religion. While many of us might find the claims of Oelschlaeger somewhat extended at times, he is on the mark in claiming that "religious discourse remains, across the spectrum of religious belief, a second language, a *language of the heart* that speaks to purposes and gives voice to issues outside the modern materialistic vocabulary of utilitarian individualism."[17] While our first language is controlled by self-interest, our second language can counter it and achieve redirection toward the commonweal. Religion can set a new agenda and bring about solidarity in the effort to achieve it. In addition to enshrining an "alternative consciousness," "religion powerfully promotes social cohesion and sentiments of common belonging."[18] It can enable us to live together in a different world, one in which sustainability overrides consumption.

An "alternative consciousness" is meaningless without an "alternative community," an institutionalized counterculture.[19] A radical break with a prevailing social reality occurs because a people center themselves on a new set of myths, metaphors, and symbols. But utilitarian individualism will not be offset just because persons begin to think differently. A paradigm shift occurs when the language of the commonweal is authorized in a community and through that community in the society at large. Berger and Neuhaus call these communities "mediating structures," which are "those institutions standing between the individual in his private life and the large institutions of public life."[20] While other institutions might be thought of, our concern with liberation theology leads us to the church, which, if it preserves the biblical tradition, is an appropriate agency of resistance to our first language.

History, Nature, and Jesus

If the church and its message are to realize their potential as a second language in relation to the environment, the Jesus event will have to be reconceived. Yet all that makes the Jesus event both central and defining for Christian theology would appear to be so focused on history that nature remains confined to the roles of setting and illustration. That problem is intensified for liberation theologians; their disposition is to treat the event as a significant replay of the Exodus. Both stories illumine the presence of God in human history as a liberator. While the incarnation may be a more intrusive event than the agency of Moses, the source of deliverance is the same. God hears the cry of God's people and responds with liberating activity. One meaning of the Jesus event is that liberation is ongoing and unambiguously historical. God is one with oppressed people and there is no salvation apart from deliverance from the power of alien forces. Nature is evident in the Exodus and at the very least illustrative for Jesus, but there is no obvious transition from historical liberation to ecological justice. Indeed, most of our worries about the tension between liberation theology and the ecocrisis are magnified by the focus on Jesus. Once again, history seems to gain ascendance over nature as the location of divine acts.

It would be a distortion, however, to suggest that Jesus was as indifferent to the natural order as most of us are. More than we, nature was an instrument of his teachings. His parables frequently draw their forcefulness from invoking the natural order. The settings are often focused on how we produce with the help of nature. What better illustration than the parable of the sower and the seed? Jesus also uses nature to define himself and his situation. "Foxes have holes, and birds of the air have nests; but the son of man has nowhere to lay his head" (Matthew 8:20). In the upper room, when the disciples gathered with Jesus for the last time, he used very basic products from nature transformed by human labor—bread and wine—to represent his life and mission. Richard C. Austin rather eloquently features the intertwining of Jesus and the natural order: "Jesus began his public life by asking John the Baptist to immerse him in the Jordan River. . . . When Jesus retreated into the wilderness to ponder his strategy, the wild beasts drew near him. He entered Peter's boat and the fish schooled about it. On his way to purify the temple, he asked the fig tree to manifest faith in a covenant renewed."[21] At the very least, Jesus was earth-friendly in the best senses. But that does not quite get us where we need to be; too often it at least sounds personal; we need something more institutional.

One dimension of the biblical tradition might seem to present itself as helpful in resolving our concerns. This is "the year of Jubilee" as evident in the twenty-fifth chapter of Leviticus. Here one finds a recognition of the need for liberation in history *and* in nature. The Jubilee year is a call to justice invoked by releasing persons, land, and property from the notion of possession. It is a reminder that everything belongs to God and any semblance of ownership is provisional: "In every seventh year, the landscape itself was freed to grow wild, slaves were given freedom, and debts were canceled."[22] Those who were impoverished and oppressed were given a fresh start and the land itself was open to renewal. Here it is clear that the Hebrew writers understood that justice embraces both history and nature. They understood that the land could become a slave just as easily as a human being could.

The connection between the Hebrew tradition and Jesus rests in part on the temple event when he read from Isaiah, chapter 61. Jesus is identifying his mission with "Good news to the poor," "release to the captives," "recovering sight to the blind," "set at liberty (the) . . . oppressed," "and to proclaim the acceptable year of Jahweh." According to John Howard Yoder, those who listened to Jesus would have understood the last phrase as referring to the Jubilee year, "the time when the inequities accumulated through the years are to be crossed off and all God's people [and the land] will begin again at some point."[23] Jesus is representing himself as having a mission for both justice on the earth and justice in relation to it.

We ought not to dismiss Jesus' relationship with nature or the accounts of Jubilee year as marginal to our concerns. They certainly stand in the way of arguing that the Jesus event is so historical that the natural order is eclipsed. But we would like to focus on an argument that may be instrumental in both positions, and therefore more fundamental, and that is the claim that Jesus is the embodiment of an ecological vision. In the first century sustainability and the related concepts we have affirmed would be alien language, but their meaning would be consistent with the metabolism of the Jesus event. "The lens of ecology" is one that gives priority to relationships and the recognition that at best everything is related and interdependent. Interconnection is the operative reality. At one level we might sustain an impulse that identifies the Jesus event with divisiveness; occasions come to mind, even in relation to his own mother, that appear to advocate disconnection. Indeed, "turning against" is an offshoot of discipleship even as Jesus' inevitable confrontation with the state shows. "Drawing lines in the sand" would seem to follow from attachment to the Jesus event. And rightly so. If one values mutuality, then one will be set apart from and against who and whatever privileges hierarchy, dualism, and individualism. Those are manifestations of a vision that is not relational, mutual, and communal.

One of the ways in which some scholars mend the nature/history fissure is by calling forth a tradition that links Jesus with creation. Earlier we noted how Jürgen Moltmann joined the creative work of God with

God's redemptive activity. He sees the Jesus event as on a continuum with God's work of creation. Sean McDonagh wants us to imagine a cosmic Christ who "was active before time in bringing forth creation."[24] He understands Colossians 1:16–17 to mean that "from the initial glow of the flaring forth, through the shaping of the elements in the cauldron of the stars and the positioning of the earth in a way that allowed it to become the green planet of the universe, right up to the emergence of humans.... [This is a story] centered on Jesus."[25] Beyond that he wants us to understand the Resurrection as an event that "renews all creation" and draws everything into "a profound relationship with the risen Lord."[26]

Denis Edwards, in *Jesus the Wisdom of God,* is more systematic and focuses the activity of God in creation through the wisdom tradition. Beginning with the Hebrew Scriptures, he traces Divine Wisdom as present in original and continuing creation. It is Edwards's contention that "wisdom is concerned with the whole of creation, and with the interrelationship among human beings, the rest of creation and God."[27]

Wisdom, Sophia, "is God's presence to the universe in continuous creation."[28] Following through the Gospels and Paul, Edwards maintains that Jesus is the incarnation of Sophia[29] and therefore is bound to the natural order in its origination and in its ongoing development. Hence, the Creator and Savior are one; history and nature are fused in the Christ event. An ecological consciousness springs from the central figure in the Christian tradition.

The arguments to which we have drawn attention above may evoke different responses from those who locate themselves within the Hebrew-Christian tradition. However, they remind us that what is really arbitrary in light of the long scriptural tradition is our assumption that Jesus is a singularly historical event, at best only marginally related to nature. Jesus is in and with the creative activity of God and its ongoing preservation. And as surely as liberation theologians understand joining Jesus in the life of the poor we can understand ourselves as joining Jesus, the embodiment of the gentle God of life, in empowering nature to be what it is and in resisting its degradation.

In an earlier chapter we referred to the claim that human beings are "children of dust and spirit"; we are nature and more; nature is in us and we are in nature. When we understand this, the incarnation has a larger meaning. When Jesus takes on our reality, both nature and history are invaded. That he became one of us means he became one with the natural order simultaneously. Karen Baker-Fletcher says it boldly: "Jesus' flesh, like the flesh of humankind, was made up of the elements that form our planet, our entire biosphere—earth, water, wind, heat. Jesus identifies not only with the sufferings and joys of being human, but with the sufferings and joys of all creation." And she concludes, "we see Jesus in the face of the earth."[30] The incarnation of God in Jesus becomes, then, a centering of the event in the spheres of history and nature, perichoretically related. Far from distancing us from nature, the Jesus event takes us more deeply into it and into an embrace of a God who redeems the cosmos, who makes "all things new."

It may help illumine our contention about the Jesus event to connect it with a notion of sin. Sin can be understood as "turning away . . . from interdependence" and "the refusal of relationship."[31] One might think of it as privileging a person or a part of the world in a way that divides and separates. Sin is being out of interconnection and interdependence. It is living or valuing according to private interests and elevating them above the common good. An ecological interpretation of sin might be rendered as ignoring sustainability, refusing an ecological vision, and repudiating everything perichoresis calls for. When James Cone writes that "to be in sin means to deny the community,"[32] he is of course referring to the human community. But when we remember that our argument has been one in which the community is seen with a perichoretic vision and includes nature in both its human and nonhuman dimensions, his definition points in the direction of our claims. Sin is abstracting ourselves "from the web" of nature to engage in domination, exploitation, and idolatry.

We are arguing that the Jesus event is one of mending and healing, restoring things in "rightful relationship." Insofar as the Jesus event is representative of the nature of God's activity, it is liberating from all that sets apart and sets over; it restores a symbiotic network. That has all the play on historical oppression that liberation theologians have traditionally claimed, but it drives beyond that to mutuality and interdependence "of all that is." There is nothing in the life, ministry, and death of Jesus that makes nature an object; indeed, we have suggested Jesus related to nature as a subject, as an integral part of his world. Indeed, the incarnation of God in Jesus is bifocal; it involves both history and nature. Jesus is with and in *everything* that is marginalized in our world, including the world itself. As Sallie McFague writes, "Surely in our time, the natural world is joined in its oppression with Christ: it too is being crucified. Just as in the face of a suffering child, woman, or man, Christians see the face of Christ, so also there is a trace of that face in a clear-cut forest, an inner-city landfill, or a polluted river."[33]

What places Jesus as focal for our ecocrisis is the embodiment of mutuality, interdependence, and connection in the whole event. We are suggesting that the essence of the Jesus event is more than its historical moorings and becomes central for establishing the priority of connection. In this framework, it is entirely appropriate to affirm, "apart from the earth there is no salvation"[34] as the preeminent form of inclusiveness.

Deconstruction and Reconstruction of Economics

It has to be significant when John Cobb, a theologian passionately concerned with environmental issues for decades, concludes "that the course of events on the planet is primarily determined by the economy . . . and that until economic thinking was changed, other changes would have minimal effect . . . standard economic theory . . . must be challenged."[35] For the role of religion to be executed and the voice of the church's message to be heard, they must be collated with a deconstruction and reconstruction of economics. That requires a challenge to the conventional wisdom of the discipline.

Neoclassical economics is presumed to focus on the behavior of the individual decision maker. The institutional arrangement of the competitive market structure is then supposed to translate that individual behavior into societal well-being. There is no provision for an analysis that places the interests of the ecological community rather than the individual human at the center of the economic matrix. Nature is only instrumental, never valued in its own right. At one level, this anthropocentrism is understandable: human beings are the only members of the community who make explicitly economic decisions.

We pointed out earlier that Adam Smith, often identified as the founder of modern economics, was interested in the connection between the economic system and the welfare of the society; he made the claim that attempts to enhance societal welfare by directly pursuing communal as opposed to individual well-being were doomed to failure. That is the essence of his discussion of the "invisible hand." The reality is that economics builds on some assumptions about what it means to pursue one's own self-interest. Those assumptions include the notion that "self-interest" and "well-being" are primarily material in nature. That is, society values material abundance above all else. Therefore, rational individuals pursuing their self-interest will do so in a context where material abundance is the principal goal. Assuming an unfettered, truly competitive environment, those individuals will not only achieve their own personal material well-being but will simultaneously maximize societal material well-being.

In doing economic analysis, we often forget the critical role played by what society values in this model. For example, what would happen if we assumed that society valued sustainability more than material abundance? Would that not also affect the goal of individual well-being? Another way to say that is to argue that what individuals desire is those things that the society values. Smith is partially right when he contends that individuals ought to pursue their own well-being rather than trying to achieve some sort of global societal welfare. In trying to do what is best for the society, one often imposes one's own will on other individuals, and uses resources to keep one's own vision front and center. Those are typically resources that could be better used in providing for satisfaction of the goal rather than maintaining the vision. But in affirming the individual in this way, we should not lose sight of the fact that the things the person chooses to pursue to satisfy self-interest are the things that he or she has learned to value as part of the socialization process of the community. Any trip to the mall will confirm that our economic decisions involve not just material goods in general, but the particular kinds of material goods that are currently in fashion. The mall is programmed to create wants, and we are conditioned to respond.

Reformers, intent upon eliminating the evils of the economic system, often want to change that system without really changing the goals that it serves. For example, they want to continue to pursue material abundance, but make sure that no one gets left out. So they leave material abundance at the center of the system and tinker with the distribution of income by means of tax-and-transfer programs. Not surprisingly, the individuals in the system are often quite dissatisfied with the outcome of this. The tax-and-transfer system is said to reduce incentives, and that leads to inefficiency in the pursuit of material abundance. At the same time, the primacy of material abundance leads many individuals to try to subvert the intent of the tax-and-transfer programs, leading to widening disparity in income distribution.

Most such "solutions" are attempts to reform the system from a position of power, and they often fail because the reform never really gets at the source of the power that sustains the status quo. We have claimed that the shared economic powerlessness of the oppressed, the laboring class, and the middle class derives from the fact that production decisions are under the control of a small group that owns and/or controls the means of production. Indeed, it is just such conditions that create environmental racism. Virtually none of the "reforms" put in place by well-meaning members of this elite have the result of changing or broadening the base for production decision making. Consequently, we continue to produce the same kinds of goods and services in the same way. In terms of our current focus on sustainability, it seems unlikely that things will be changed in any significant way if we leave the changing up to the current elite, who derive all of their benefits from the existing patterns of production and consumption. Think of annual attempts at tax reform as a useful analogy. Most such attempts are proposed by members of a political leadership who may really want to build a better and more equitable tax system. Yet the reality is that any such reform, before it gets put in place, gets riddled with provisions, exemptions, and exceptions designed to protect the positions and reduce the tax liability of at least some of those who belong to the political and economic elite.

Reforms will also be relatively ineffective until and unless the values inherent in the reform become central to the mission of the society. There must be congruence between what we believe is important and what we decide to do. Virtually everyone in U.S. society understands and subscribes to the goal of material abundance. Relatively speaking, only a small part of the population understands and accepts sustainability as a goal. It is not surprising, then, that when the society engages in production and consumption most of the effort is directed toward material growth; as a result, sustainability is largely ignored.

Real change involves two things. First, it must be proposed and implemented by those who do not have power in the conventional sense because, having nothing idiosyncratic to protect, they will be willing to entertain fundamental as opposed to cosmetic change. Second, the change must rest on a base of widely shared social values. The first point means that significant environmental change can come about only as a result of a grassroots movement, a coalition of the lower and middle classes, drawing on the communal power inherent in their shared powerlessness. The second point means that no such grassroots movement will be successful until it is drawing upon a shared vision of societal well-being that looks through an ecological lens and includes sustainability as a central tenet.

Imagine, for the moment, that the neoclassical economic analysis is accurate: individuals do aggressively pursue their own self-interest in their economic actions. But also assume that most individuals see sustainability as an essential thread in the fabric of societal welfare. It seems unlikely that such individuals would, in pursuing their own self-interest, choose a pattern of consumption that was highly polluting if they could avoid it. That argument fits with Smith's claims about the invisible hand. The unspoken factor that makes the Smithian analysis work is that the goals of the individuals and the goal of society are parallel—the individual tries to maximize personal material well-being and the society tries to maximize overall material well-being. A real change in society's shared measure of welfare most likely would be reflected in the vision of personal welfare held by most individuals. We can turn the parallelism in a slightly different direction: If the society is trying to maximize overall *sustainable* material well-being, then the individual will be trying to maximize personal *sustainable* material well-being.

This twist to the analysis does not, by any means, get us to a new vision of the economic system. There is still an analytic mystery surrounding what shape the economic system will take under this new set of assumptions about goals. That is, what kinds of economic decisions will get made and how will they be made? The society must also figure out how to inculcate sustainability as an essential thread in the measurement of societal welfare. There is one other difficulty, and it is not a new one. We have already detailed why, in our current economic system, pursuit of individual goals does not always translate into societal welfare because of concentration of power, market imperfections, and market failure. While sustainability provides a new set of boundary conditions within which the market can operate, it does not eliminate the possibilities for concentration, imperfection, and failure—any and all of which can subvert the sustainability goal as easily as they currently subvert the material abundance goal.

The first task is to hypothesize about new forms of analysis. We suggested in the introduction to this chapter that privileging an ecological vision would demand that the society value and uphold an "ecological trinity" of community, mutuality, and connectedness. We have also said that any "new" economic system will still involve individuals actively pursuing their own self-interest, but that self-interest will be defined differently. One aspect of the different definition would be that an ecological community would reshape self-interest. For example, if the socialization process led to a community that defined enhanced well-being as a communal rather than an individual goal, persons would not be likely to see any action as being in their self-interest if it in some way damaged the community. This could clearly change the decisions they make, but would it change the process by which decisions are made?

There are two fundamental kinds of decisions that individuals make in the economic system, the decision to consume goods and services and the decision to produce goods and services. The first decision involves balancing all the possible consumption decisions and their associated prices against one another. In a perfect world the prices of each good or service would reflect all of the costs involved in producing and using that good, including any associated environmental effects. And if there is concern for community-informed self-interest, then the utility or well-being that the consumer gets from that good or service would also reflect its environmental impact. So, while the information people used in making consumption decisions would be more extensive, the process would not change. Individual consumers would still be balancing their choices of goods and services in an effort to maximize individual utility.

The decision about what and how much to produce involves the business firm in the process of maximizing profit subject to constraints on the cost and availability of resources. On the consumer side, it was easy to say "if the prices reflected all of the environmental costs," but the producer side is where those environmental costs get loaded in. Daly's depletion quotas could be used to ensure that the prices of inputs of raw materials adequately reflected the environmental cost of providing those materials. What is not so clear is what mechanisms would ensure that the environmental costs of the production process itself were reflected in the prices of goods and services. Accounting for the damages increases the cost of production and reduces profit, so there is no a priori reason why the producer would be eager to make such an accounting. The argument on the consumer's side is that the individual's choices would be so informed by a communal ethic that environmentally damaging consumption would yield less utility than environmentally friendly consumption. Thus the goal of maximizing utility would be directly affected by the inculcation of a communal value attached to sustainability.

There is no comparable effect on the producer, since profit is an objective dollar amount of return on investment rather than a subjective measure of well-being. That is, on the consumer's side, utility will be affected *because* there is environmental damage from consumption, and that lowers the satisfaction one gets from the consumption activity. Profit, on the other hand, will not be affected *unless* the producer incorporates environmental costs into the production process. There is nothing inherent in the process to encourage the producer to make this change, and so the process itself will have to be changed in order to ensure environmentally responsive production decisions. We think that it is important to see that a change in values—the elevation of community and the inculcation of a perichoretic ecological vision—is necessary, and may be sufficient to get consumption behavior reoriented toward building sustainability. However, while such a change is necessary on the production side, it is not sufficient. In addition, there must be institutional restructuring as well. Daly's depletion quotas are one example of new institutional arrangements. There must be similar institutional restructuring in terms of the environmental impact of the production process itself. Creation of standards and regulations is, of course, one way that our contemporary society tries to accomplish this. But it would be better and more socially beneficial if the ecological lens so shaped our behavior that incentives were created to make the pursuit of profit by producers congruent with the pursuit of ecological well-being.

We have identified the need to embrace sustainability and argued that it would be prudent for the individual in community. But the primacy of sustainability is not sufficiently assured by "what makes sense." We need to move deeper and ask how a community might begin to embrace sustainability as normal and in a sense instinctive. That forces us to consider more specifically both the kinds of mediating institutions we need and the concrete steps that must be taken to create them. That institutionalization of the "ecological trinity" is the subject of our final chapter.

S·I·X

Implementing the New Order

If one visits Granville, Massachusetts, it is not difficult to imagine why pioneering emigrants from there settled where they did in Ohio. The Welsh Hills, fertile land, and running streams in their new home spoke to the hand and the soul alike. The settlers came with a plan to nestle into nature in ways that respected its gifts. Those of us who have come after them, more than a century and a half later, have not always planned as carefully or respectfully. Farm lands and wooded areas yielded to housing and commercial projects as developers' financial resources proved irresistible. Displaced animals soon became the enemy of the "civilized"; recently, one councilperson even proposed legislation making it legal to shoot deer inside the village limits. Invasive highways on the edge of our community competed with the sounds of nature and soon there were calls for speedier access and services. Some called it inevitable progress; they were usually ones who benefited in the coinage of the land. But many others, bewildered and numbed by that "progress," slowly realized that the very small-village qualities they enjoyed were on the cusp of extinction.

It took a petition drive and a ballot issue mandating a six-month moratorium on commercial construction to bring the community to attention about the loss of their way of life. And we—parents and merchants, academics and professionals, short- and long-term residents— found ourselves in motion. Other words by Alice Walker, words less whimsical and mystical, identified our agenda: "Helped are those who find the courage to do at least one small thing each day to help the existence of another—plant, animal, river, human being. They shall be joined by a multitude of the timid."[1] Even if we shift our focus to a reconceived common good, it will still take the mobilization of a "multitude of the timid" to save the environment, including the small piece of it that is Granville, Ohio.

In our village or elsewhere, when we respond to our needs and wants in ways that do not limit the ability of future generations to provide for theirs, we are participating in sustainability. But that is not a sufficient answer to the ecocrisis; it does not move us decisively beyond anthropocentrism. Sustainability is the form our restraint can take in our use of the natural order, and were we to embrace it, holocaustic devastation would be arrested. The more fundamental and radical agenda, however, is the sensibility that emerges from our ecological lens and invokes mutuality, connection, and community. The emergence of a "dominant consciousness" that affirms the intrinsic interdependence of everything is at the heart of an ecological transformation.

For that to happen, an ecological vision must seek political and economic form; churches must become communities that celebrate in ritual a perichoretic vision; and a reconception of the good life must occur, centered on the service of the common good.

The Ecological Trinity and Its Implementation

Religious "language of the heart," the Jesus event as the restoration of "rightful relationship," and a reconception of economic theory call out for supporting institutional structures; indeed, without some evident system the sentiments they represent wither and die.

The most obvious structural reality is that existing institutions have been created by and to some extent exist within communities, or social groups. The spirit of perichoresis that we want to inculcate leads us to the consideration of alternative political communities and the explicit forms they might take. For example, narrowly focused utopian communities have an attractive history of creating cooperative political systems based on consensus building. But, in practice, they have seldom had much effect on the wider society. For example, the Oneida community, nineteenth-century Owenite communities like New Harmony, or Koinonia Farms founded by Clarence Jordan all were interesting challenges to the status quo for a while, but there is scant evidence that the experiments have been imitated, and often the communities faded as their founders grew older or as the demands of the economic system overwhelmed them. We are convinced that society as a whole encompasses far too diverse a set of players, needs, and goals to allow a consensual system to operate effectively.

Democratic systems would seem to have an edge in creating the appropriate responses to environmental issues, since they are already set to listen to a broad spectrum of input. Yet extant democratic systems are particularly responsive to concentrations of power, not to the voice of the other. Voting blocs and concentrations of income and wealth are the typical forms in which power is concentrated and exercised. Democratic political systems that are exceptionally pluralistic do exist, but they tend to be characterized by limited effectiveness and, occasionally, chaos.

On the other hand, existing authoritarian systems have been even worse in their failure to respond to environmental concerns. They seem to have the concentrated power but not the political will to be ecosensitive. Each of these disparate political systems has failed to address adequately the degradation of nature. What we need is a political structure that has the effective power of authoritarian systems, the widespread input possibilities of democracy, and the sharing of power and decision making found in consensus-based systems.

As we have argued, the dominant economic systems are conspicuously inadequate when it comes to the environment. To parallel the political system we have suggested, a viable economic structure would have to make its decisions in response to a wide variety of inputs, have the effective power to make and enforce decisions, and share the decision-making power widely. In most economic systems, power rests with the ownership and/or control over the use of productive resources, particularly land, mineral resources, and capital. Whatever the ostensible form of an economic system, control over the use of resources rests with wealth and income. A system that hopes to be effective in creating sustainable development and recognizing nature as a category of analysis has two alternatives. It must either find another avenue for the expression and implementation of power, or discover a different and sustainable way to redistribute wealth and income so that the power to make and enforce decisions is diffused. In any event, power and wealth as traditionally conceived cannot go unchallenged.

One difficulty that critics of the status quo always face is the problem of adequately discussing and describing alternatives to the present system. There is a dominant language, a first language, which often restricts our discussions of changes in politics and economics to variations of the current order. This use of the dominant language makes it difficult to describe any set of institutions that is different from and counter to the existing system. In the last chapter we discussed the necessity of creating a second language, a language of the heart, to counter the utilitarian individualism of our first language. Thinking of God as the "gentle God of life," and seeing Jesus as the embodiment of an ecological vision, generates that language for us. It finds expression in an ecological trinity of mutuality, connectedness, and community. The emergence of those values could be used to shape alternative political and economic structures. *Mutuality* places importance on shared interests and on the achievement of shared goals. *Connectedness* stresses relationships; it suggests that decision making ought to focus on sturdy resistance to sacrificing the well-being of one for the interests of another. *Community,* however, carries both mutuality and connectedness a step further by insisting that all decisions reflect a broad base of support and the interests of the whole ecosystem.

In suggesting the shape of a system that is driven by and honors the ecological trinity, it is tempting to claim that a particular alternative structure would be "like" socialism, or "like" capitalism. In an earlier discussion, we outlined some of the benefits and problems associated with each system. But using either or both as our model is just a way to envision a system that is an evolutionary extension of those extant systems that we know about and are comfortable with. We might indeed draw many analogies between some emerging alternative economic and political systems and those that already exist; however, analogy and familiarity ought not to provide the limits for our analysis. Instead, we need to think about structures in terms of their contribution to mutuality, connectedness, and community. It makes little difference for the parts to sound familiar and comfortable while the whole is organized in destructive ways. In fact, there is at least one very good reason to avoid the familiar in the early stages of this analysis; all existing systems are to some significant degree hierarchical, and that does not work very well as we strive to effect mutuality and an inclusive community.

What political and economic structures would be mutual, relational, and focused on the community rather than hierarchical and centered on the individual? While political and economic power *are* interrelated, they are not relational. That is, extant systems tend to reinforce the unequal and inequitable distribution of power to individuals and groups, and the use of that power to serve their interests, rather than thinking about power as a tool for accomplishing the well-being of the whole society. Therefore, in any society that holds up connectedness and relationship as dominant values, we should expect differences in both the distribution of power and the use of power. With our first language, it is hard to conceive of power outside of its use to achieve the goals of utilitarian individualism. But relational power is different: it comes from relationships; it arises from the shared vision of the community and is used to serve the shared needs.

Mutuality calls for an end to hierarchy and the beginning of establishing the voice and place of the "other," whether that other is other persons, future generations, or nature; it stresses the ecological "we" rather than the human "I." Power in service of mutuality can become a reality if the preferential option for the environment becomes an overarching value for the society. Finally, an effective alternative society must find ways to use power that are an expression of broadly based communal interests.

While there are many structures that shape and express the dominant values of a society, we want to concentrate our attention on the political and economic structures that directly reflect and create the distribution and use of power in the society. At some fundamental level, our existing political institutions stress differences because that is how they mobilize political support—Republicans vs. Democrats, conservatives vs. liberals, Washington "insiders" vs. "Middle America"; and, in the more strident language of some, the middle class vs. welfare recipients, white vs. black, male vs. female, the environment vs. jobs. If we want the institutional arrangements to embody mutuality, then we must develop political institutions that eschew such differences and stress shared interests instead. It is our contention, for example, that poverty among the "lower" classes and powerlessness among the "middle" classes stem from the same root cause: their inability to control the circumstances of their lives owing to the concentration of political and economic power among a small elite. When we look at the world through an ecological lens it is easier to see that we need political coalitions that empower the marginalized, including nature and future generations. If that same power came into play in the economic world, it would demand that production decisions be the result of decision making that is shared. And the sharing should include more than those with a direct material interest such as workers, management, and consumers; mutuality calls for a broader decision-making community that includes the representatives of nature and the future, those who are most likely to be affected by any externalities arising from the production decisions. That is a way of beginning to institute a counterculture, creating an alternative community that expresses a new consciousness and draws upon a second language. For example, imagine that under our present structures, a business buys a piece of property and decides to build a new plant. Its decision is presumptively valid unless members of the surrounding human community present compelling arguments for setting aside the property rights of the business. The outcome is often long and expensive litigation and temporary paralysis of the system. What if the initial decision-making process involved a wider range of decision makers who embodied mutuality and connectedness? While there are no guarantees, it seems reasonable that the process could then be accomplished and serve the broad interests of the human and natural community more effectively.

When connectedness is the focus, emerging political coalitions must begin to recognize the folly of single-issue politics without surrendering to the emptiness of "something for everyone." We could adopt the language of the U.S. Catholic bishops when they call for a "consistent ethic of life," the "seamless web" of connectedness that we identified earlier. Their emphasis is not broad enough for our purposes because it does not explicitly include nature. The "God of life" calls us to move beyond that; it calls for political coalitions to exercise their power and bring about the passage of legislation that is life-affirming in the broadest possible sense, that is, giving scope to the fullest possibilities and the widest diversities of life and life forms. Such an approach recognizes all the interactions, both life-affirming and life-denying, that occur when any particular course of political action is chosen.

Economically, connectedness forces us to recognize that trade-offs are real. Making any decision to use resources in a certain way *will* have consequences in terms of the quality of life of this generation, the quality of the environment for this and future generations, the possibilities for economic choice for future generations, and the survivability of other species that utilize those same resources. That means that we cannot rely on one-dimensional systems to make economic decisions in the hope that they will clearly account for all of the trade-offs—private, social, and natural—that are connected with any allocation, production, or consumption decision. While the market can account effectively for some effects, central planning for others, and cost-benefit analysis for still others, no single type of system is capable of monitoring and responding to all of the interconnected needs involved in bringing about sustainable development for a naturocentric community.

The kind of community we envision can engender political and economic structures that will drive us toward choices that reflect broad-based communal interests rather than narrow elite-dominated desires. One of the political difficulties faced by the contemporary environmental movement is that the solutions its proponents advocate reflect only a limited sense of mutual interests along with a concern for connection; they have an incomplete sense of community that excludes those with economic interests; as a result, they do not envision solutions that will both reflect and win broad-based support. The emergence of eco-terrorists and terrorism against eco-activists both reflect the failure to think in terms of community. The controversy around which the spotted owl issue was built is a good example of that. Using existing political mechanisms and mobilizing a network of activists, the environmental movement has halted lumber development in some areas of the Northwest in order to protect the habitat of the owl. The problem is that their support base is largely other environmental activists. Using that base as a source for their solutions does not allow a broad enough range to encompass the very real and very human economic issues that drive the pressure for forest development. Building a different kind of political coalition that included both the environmental and the economic interests might engender a different but still ecologically desirable political policy.

This is one of the places where it is possible to suggest some economic institutional arrangements that can provide significant help in driving the system toward more appropriate and broadly based input and outcomes. A system of widespread social ownership of the means of production could wrench the production process away from its overweening emphasis on private profit and redirect its efforts toward societal good. That is, after all, one of the claims for socialism. It is also possible, however, that a similar redirection could be accomplished by a dramatic increase in the dispersion of private ownership. Concentrated individual private ownership in an era of uncertainty about future use of resources is very likely to lead to excessive current exploitation and a consequent reduction in future productivity. For example, large oil companies have a vested interest in the use of oil and the profit that flows from that; they certainly are not overly concerned about the negative consequences of its use on nature and the environment. They operate in a world dominated by utilitarian individualism, and what they want is more wealth and profit, however they can get it. But since they so dominate the markets in which they operate, they feel little pressure even to be efficient in the exploitation of petroleum resources, let alone think about managing those resources in ways that respect mutuality, connectedness, and community. Even within a market context, a more widely spread net of ownership, with many more producers, would create the opportunity for the community to call individual producers to task when they fail to respect the needs and interests of community.

We can briefly summarize our political arguments. In the political sphere, an appropriate and effective system will need to have at least three broad interdependent groups represented and empowered in the political decision-making process: all currently living human beings, future generations of human beings, and nature. This is a large step, since all current political systems, at best, empower only a small part of the currently living human beings, leaving all other members of the ecosystem relatively powerless.

But it is not enough to have representation and some empowerment; a new system will also need to find ways to negotiate the interests of all in a political process that leads to decisions that adequately reflect the needs of the whole community. Finally, out of such a diversified decision-making environment, the system must also find ways to focus power so that decisions can be enacted. Unfocused power leads to anarchy and gridlock. The powerless have to be empowered—through their mutual, reciprocal, and symbiotic relationships—in ways that lead to effective communal decision making.

Thus far we have intentionally placed most of our emphasis on the political decision-making structures because the economic decision-making process is in some ways derived from the political one. Until the community sets its goals, the economist cannot define the path. Using the language of utilitarian individualism, economists often claim that their only function is that of effective resource management; the ultimate purpose of that management is a political goal. That is, there must often be a declaration of the political will to accomplish some goal, especially one that involves significant change, before it is possible to muster the economic resources needed to fulfill the goal. If our language centers on mutuality, connectedness, and community, then the goals become different and they call for a different kind of economic system; enacting the perichoretic political will cannot be accomplished with the individual economic model.

An effective alternative economic system first needs a complete inventory of the human and nonhuman resources actually and potentially available. Second, it needs a system or systems for making allocation decisions so that current generations, future generations, and nature make equitable contributions to the resource base and have an equitable access to the use and enjoyment of the resources. Finally, power will need to be focused to turn such allocation decisions into reality.

It is important to note that "power" is an important word in the discussion of both political and economic systems. Recall, for example, our discussion about the welfare implications of concentrated economic power in chapter 2. There we claimed that the powerful were able to accomplish their goals within the economic system whether or not those goals served the welfare of the whole society. In a real sense, building an ecologically viable future for planet Earth and all of its species calls for the power, the goals, and social welfare to all line up. Accomplishing that requires the empowering of the powerless, including nature. In fact, it is probably not possible to move very far toward that future until the empowering occurs. Empowering is both a political and an economic act. To use an analogy once again, it is clear that blacks and women in the United States have discovered that emerging political voice without improved economic well-being and control is a hollow sham that mocks real change. The effective political power to set societal goals and the effective economic power to move appropriate resources in order to fulfill those goals must come together, or neither will be accomplished. From the perspective of building an ecologically viable future, current political and economic structures are all saddled with concentrated rather than dispersed power and competitive rather than cooperative use of that power. Any new structural arrangements must address those power issues and rearrange those power concentrations. In the last section of this chapter, we intend to discuss more fully the kind of economic system that might emerge from an institutional framework that elevated a community of mutuality.

In the previous chapter we showed how the Judeo-Christian tradition can yield a privileged position for an ecological vision. We are persuaded that privileging an ecological vision could set in motion a whole set of institutional changes. Shifting away from the language of individualism and driving toward mutuality, connectedness, and community has helped us to translate that vision into new possibilities and new forms for the political and economic systems. And this is a process in which the institution of the church can play a significant role in socializing people into a perichoretic consciousness and a new approach to the common good.

The Role of the Church

The separation of church and state has a long and tortured history. Stephen L. Carter shows how that doctrine has been distorted to exclude the claims of faith from the public square and confine them to the private realm.[2] But there has never been a claim for the separation of church and nature! Whether that is because the church has been perceived to be innocuous in relation to nature or just plain irrelevant need not be resolved here. Our concern is with arguing that the church, as the institutionalization of one religion, is integral in U.S. society to transforming our relationship to nature. It may be our "last, best hope."

Wolfhart Pannenberg argues that "the Christian church is a symbolic community" and beyond that "the community itself is symbolic."[3] Symbols do not have a life of their own; they exist in communities even as communities are created by them. All communities deal in symbols; symbols define a community as well as articulate its sense of reality. Part of what distinguishes the church at its most authentic is that it is the venue where symbols clash and are held in tension. The church is the place where the symbols of the biblical tradition may confront the symbols of the society. Some will remind us of the phenomenon of "enculturation." The church at times not only embraces the values of the "dominant consciousness," but lends its symbols to another agenda. Nazi Germany and South Africa under apartheid are extreme examples of a cultural captivity of the church's message. But the task of the church is "to bring the claims of the tradition and the situation of enculturation into an effective interface."[4]

In our discussion of metaphors for God and Jesus' relationship to nature we have been attempting to use the lens of ecology to reclaim the tradition for mutuality, connectedness, and community rather than utilitarian individualism. What we now are contending is that the church, the community of faith, is an appropriate place for the dialogue between our first and second languages to occur. Our first language is the one generated in and encultured by modern individual-centered communities; the second is the language of tradition, further shaped by the ecological trinity, and used by faith communities. Specifically, the church is a suitable locus for a debate: the alliance of growth, greed, and consumption that imposes extensive costs on the environment vs. the recognition that history, nature, and God exist in a perichoretic relationship. The church can be the source of criticism and resistance to the prevailing order in its affirmation of the second language. In the clash of symbols, the church can be a midwife in the "culture-forming power of the biblical outlook."[5] As such, the church is instrumental in transforming a consciousness that is anthropocentric and establishing one in which nature has intrinsic value in an inclusive community. One of the roles of the symbols of faith is to elevate a sense of the common good that will wean us away from utilitarian individualism and enable us to bond with "all that is." In the imagery of Sallie McFague, we can understand our place in "the Body of God."

Viewing the church as the arena in which symbols of faith challenge symbols of the society suggests that the church itself is "culture-forming." It can create a new consciousness and embody its validity. Stanley Hauerwas makes a distinction between the church having a social ethic and being a social ethic, between its rhetoric and its reality.[6] He is contrasting mere pronouncements on responsibility with the existence of a community that lives that way. The church not only sets its own agenda, but it can be an earthly manifestation of it. The church exists as witness to "the peaceable kingdom," in contrast to the mendacity and malice of the world. As such the church is "a community of virtues" living in terms of a new age while the old one continues to exist.[7] What we want to argue is that the church is a "symbolic community"[8] in precisely this sense. The church can be a community of ecological virtues in which the narratives of faith are told and sacramentally enacted so that those within it are re-socialized. The kinds of abstract and seemingly disparate themes we have been articulating—absolute scarcity and sustainability—involve learned sensibilities. The gospel of greed, acquisition, and material reassurance— also learned—is countered by a community whose faith comes to focus upon an ecological existence. This means a communal life in which partnership with nature is given common expression. If Jesus is the embodiment of an ecological lens, and the incarnation constitutes a fusion of nature and history, then our metaphors for God and our sacramental practice can draw us into mutuality and the recognition that we are not just individuals or species but that our social reality can ultimately be defined only in the context of an ecological system. Earth, neighbor, self, and God all exist in relation and in balance. We come together with future generations, with the natural order, and with the tensions between growth and restraint. In worship and in common practice, the virtues of the new age are internalized and those of the old age rejected. Ecological virtues are sustained not so much by intuition, reason, or threat, but by the fact that we are with nature in a community that has established reciprocal and symbiotic relationships among all its members. Here we understand ourselves as members of the "earth community" and accept the responsibility that entails. The displacement of utilitarian individualism occurs within a community in which there is a daily celebration of the comprehensiveness of God's creation and our place within it. There "that feeling of being part of everything, not separate at all"[9] becomes defining.

We have been suggesting that the church can be a community that embodies an ecological consciousness. But beyond that, or because of it, it can also become a direct force in the economic and political spheres. It can respond to the ecocrisis by virtue of its existence as a counter-institution.

We noted earlier Douglas Meeks's argument about the failure of the Protestant church to wrestle with economic issues and the economic order. We might extend that contention by saying that while the church has a long history of spawning movements, agencies, and even institutions in areas like civil rights, peace, and health care, it has no comparable history in relation to the disorder that the prevailing economic system can impose on both the human and nonhuman parts of our ecological community. There have, of course, been cases where the church has been evident as a "counterinstitution" in the economic sphere. The social encyclicals of the popes over the last hundred years and the Catholic bishops' letter on the U.S. economy are examples of the church "speaking out." More-active involvement in the system is seen in the voting of proxies by "corporate citizens" and in the active divestiture of stock ownership as a challenge to corporate practices. But this is still activity within the system, "after the cards are dealt." What we don't see is the church actively engaged in changing the system in ways that would eliminate the causes of economic and environmental injustice.

Walter Brueggemann[10] has made a helpful distinction between the "dominant consciousness" and the "alternative consciousness" in U.S. society. While there have been times when the church became "enculturated," at its best the church has imagined itself to be an "alternative community," one that stands for realities that are missing in the prevailing order. It is not clear, however, that we have the imagination or energy to move beyond protest and belief to create the institutional shape of the church's role in a new order. To revamp an old line from a *New Yorker* cartoon, what would we do if the conventional wisdom were us? Students reading Brueggemann always imagine that if the "alternative community" became the "dominant community" it would be essentially like what had passed away. Their sense of reality is so controlled by the status quo that it is difficult for them to imagine anything else. At a pragmatic level there may be some truth to their view. But we believe their concern reveals a lack of vision and specificity on the part of those who aspire to an "alternative consciousness." This is especially true in relation to the economic order. The tendency of theologians and "church types" has been to frame the debate as capitalism vs. socialism; our friends sell out to capitalism and our enemies buy into socialism. At a time when both are "on the rocks" that may not be a very helpful way of setting the agenda!

The church can be the arena for rekindling public discussion about issues the larger society has seemingly already resolved in the spirit of utilitarian individualism, at whatever cost to the environment. Some will want to remind us that the church has at times affirmed our first language and become itself a manifestation of unbridled consumption. Obviously the church has a history of deviating from the biblical tradition, but it also has a history of fidelity. In our own time the white church in South Africa sanctioned apartheid but also facilitated the emergence of Desmond Tutu. And in the United States the church was a primary location for the civil rights movement. At its best it has been an important source of criticism and resistance to the prevailing order. There is a "culture-forming power of the biblical outlook,"[11] and the church is the community through which it happens. As we have claimed, it can be the place where a second language engages our first language and the near-fatal wounds of the environment are recognized and addressed.

We contend that the church can find specific ways of implementing an "alternative consciousness" in the economic arena, a consciousness in which the claims of justice for both human beings and nature has a prominent place. Is it not possible that the church could address economic and ecological needs as it has educational, medical, and social needs in the past? That would require us to think first about satisfying economic need and only later about the claims of property and power. In our work, we have been long on recognizing the "loveless power" of our first language, which controls the institutions of society. We have been drawn also to "powerless love" as a mode of influencing our world. And the church, at least in its rhetoric, makes the same moves. What is needed is for the church to take a leading role in bringing "love" and "power" together in the creation of structural relationships that elevate both human and environmental justice. That may have been tried at times from the vantage point of privilege, but we need to explore what it might be like to do it from the perspective of the victims.

In support of such a move, the church has at least two symbolic acts in which mutuality, connectedness, and community are visibly embodied. And in these acts the prophetic dimension is centered in the priestly function; they have the potential for being environmentally significant. Holy Communion and baptism have more often than not been seen as the agents of salvation for the individual. The bread and the wine have been understood as "the medicine of immortality"; they are the means of our personal salvation. And baptism has been understood as the portal to the sphere of salvation and the promise of a community to the person. But both sacraments have "culture-forming" power that is consequential for the natural order.

In an earlier book we argue that "the Lord's Supper was and can be a revolutionary ritual, . . . an act of political subversion. . . . Those who come to the table as biblically conceived come to resist death."[12] In support of that we argued that in its original setting, the rite of the Jewish Pasch, it was a celebration of the Exodus and God's liberation of an oppressed people. We went on to claim that "the taking of bread and wine involves the creation of mutuality."[13] At the time we only understood "mutuality" as a human bonding and communal affirmation. Ironically, we named the bread and wine without understanding their significance! We have always understood the elements as "staples of life," especially in that time. They are that, but more significantly they are nature's gifts and presence in Christianity's most sacred ritual. Our initial reaction may be that we are more apt to think of the bread and wine as coming from the local Kroger store than from the earth. In the absence of an agricultural society, "the gifts of the earth and the works of our hands" that we liturgically affirm may be empty vessels. Yet the elements of the Eucharist can be restored in our consciousness. They can "symbolically gather into themselves not only the earth, the sun, and the elements of the cosmos, but all human activity as well."[14] The bread and the wine symbolize the perichoretic relationship between earth, humankind, and God; they reaffirm the ecological trinity of mutuality, connectedness, and community.

As we noted in chapter 2, for Gutiérrez creation, salvation, and liberation are not separate and distinct acts. They converge in giving rise to a new humanism. We want to claim that God as Creator and God as Liberator and God as Savior become one in the eucharist. Those who come to the table to remember historical liberation do so with the elements of nature. What we want to contend, then, is that the sacrament of communion is a ritual that plays out an "ecological vision." It is preeminently an acting-out of and celebration of a life that embodied mutuality in consort with nature's representation in bread and wine. The historical and the natural order intersect in remembering Jesus as the one who reconnects us with God, each other, and the earth. Earlier we quoted Lappe and Callicott as saying, "Ecology reveals that organisms are not only mutually related and interdependent; they are also mutually defining."[15] The community of faith "reproduces" and "routinizes" that reality each time it participates in a sacrament that remembers the Exodus, and Jesus, through the fruits of the earth "elevated" to subject status within an inclusive community. Hierarchy is purged and we find ourselves within nature, not differentiated from it. And for a moment, "the broken web" is mended.

Nature is also affirmed in baptism. At its worst, the church has seemed to suggest that baptism is something like an inoculation received in the doctor's office. Everyone who can gain access to the shots gets them and they are to protect the child against evil diseases. For reasons it is not easy to understand, even the more secular in our society are reluctant to have an unbaptized child! You wouldn't want to put an innocent soul at risk! Baptism can mean more than "welcome to the club" and "your soul is safe with Jesus." Baptism can be understood as a means of overcoming individualism and all its anthropocentric overtures. It could in fact be an act that binds us into an appropriate relationship with nature. One of the reasons why the presence of nature in the sacrament has been lost is that it has been removed from "the river Jordan" to a fount in the sanctuary. In current practice, the element of water is less prominent; but it is still essential. What we want to suggest is that baptism need not be seen as entrusting a soul to Jesus as his follower, but as immersion in "the Body of God." And if God is the gentle God of life, then baptism can also be interpreted as entry into the perichoretic relation of God, nature, and community. No ritual more clearly states our place within nature and our reciprocity with it. Even more than communion, baptism is a rite of nature and an affirmation of our essential bond with it. We may not so readily "recognize God in the face of the living rivers"[16] but water in our time remains therapeutic, is essential to the survival of all living things, and is the agent of cleansing. And it is one thing even the most pretentious mortals cannot claim as having created! The water in baptism is a statement of solidarity and mutuality with all creation: it is essential for earth-healing and producing, and a bearer of sacred spirits.

Both sacraments can be a way of representing that we are saved/liberated through Christ by nature. The bread and the wine and the water are agents of interconnection and interrelationship. One might even say "there is no salvation outside nature." Nature is essential to our God relationship in its inception and its maintenance. Rather than a hierarchy of God, humankind, and nature, there is a triangularity in which each participates in the other. What baptism and communion have in common is the *body* of Christ and our inclusion in it. Bodies live in history, but they are nature. Rightly understood, these two sacraments subvert individualism and anthropocentrism. They represent and ritualize a new consciousness.

Pursuing the Common Good: Reconceiving the Good Life

In this book we have advocated elevating the common good over individual self-interest; we have called for the emergence of a perichoretic vision utilizing an ecological lens; and we have urged the primacy of our ecological trinity of mutuality, connectedness, and community. Within that context, the new consciousness mentioned above has to take shape; the common good requires contours. And that, in turn, calls for a reconception of the good life. Earlier we presented Weaver and Jameson's argument that every society, at least implicitly, has some conception of the good life and tries to order its political and economic institutions to achieve it. In *Habits of the Heart,* Robert Bellah et al. tried to describe what that good life might be from the perspectives of a group of diverse Americans. Their analysis argued that pursuit of individual self-interest, individualism, "may have grown cancerous."[17] But their solution calls for an end to isolation by restoring the best of our national and religious heritage. While they seem to talk about community, their appeal is, at its core, another demand for personal transformation. In contrast, when Herman Daly and John Cobb Jr. wrote *For the Common Good,* they claimed that welfare must be defined in the context of the community. Drawing upon Aristotle's *oikonomia,* they argued for the "management of the household so as to increase its use values to all members of the household over the long run."[18] The well-being of the community is more than the sum of the welfares of all the individual members of society, and it cannot be achieved just by getting our personal lives right.

We think the process of redefinition needs to be extended to encompass some additional elements. The "good life" should measure human fulfillment as something more important than material gain, and it should make ecological balance both an important part of and on an equal footing with that human fulfillment. It should recognize the potentially deleterious economic and social impact of honoring competition in a society that has less of it all the time. And the good life must be defined from the bottom up, so that it truly confronts the distortion of human values arising from the increasing disparity between the top and bottom of the income distribution. One of the reasons why faith communities are important in this process is that their symbols and practices can support a new articulation of the good life that moves us from searching for the individual good to sustaining the common good.

If the language of the new "good life" is to draw upon the vision seen through the ecological lens, then it is essential for our redefinition and the resulting actions to come from the marginalized. Both people and nature are being hurt and disadvantaged by the existing conditions, and our definition needs to grow out of that lived reality. Even though we are not the disadvantaged, we are able to suggest areas on which attention might be focused and to give some ideas about the role the church and other institutions might play in the process. The ultimate shape of change will have to arise from the needs and the anguish of people and nature, those who are being continually put down within the existing system.

If we really want to preserve nature and show respect for all life, we must move the good life away from its overwhelmingly material base and onto one in which ethical and ecological considerations restrain material consumption. Many elements in the contemporary material measurement of the good life serve symbolic rather than functional purposes. "How much" or "how many" or "what kind" seem to be more important questions than "for what purpose?" Labels and logos often seem to be more important than intrinsic quality. The advertising barrage that solidifies the importance of the labels and logos has obvious implications for the identity and sense of self-worth of the poor, who cannot afford those products. What is less obvious is the impact on nature of the wasteful production and consumption activities that surround the labels and logos. Producing too many "things" draws unnecessarily on the resource base that supports all life. Consuming too many "things" unnecessarily uses up the waste-sink and recycling capacities of the ecosphere.

Even though we want to begin in a different place, from the perspective of the victim, we agree with Daly and Cobb that pursuing a new vision of the common good requires us to rethink what kind of community we have and how important it is. When individualism is at the heart of the economic system, there is a great deal of difficulty in inculcating the values of the ecological trinity. Mutuality and connectedness can find full flower only in a world where community is at the center of our existence. And we need the emergence of those values if society is to heed the call for limits on the scale of economic activity. Rational egoism constantly pushes the individual to increase access to and use of material goods and services.

But as we have argued, increasing individual consumption does not always and necessarily improve the well-being of the society.

Daly and Cobb make that point by drawing on John Hicks's usage of the term income. Hicks argues that income should be properly understood as the amount of consumption that can be undertaken without diminishing future consumption possibilities.[19] While Hicks was certainly a proponent of rational individualism, he recognized that unrestrained pursuit of material well-being by individuals could reduce their own well-being by damaging the resource base from which they draw. That provides at least a tacit recognition of the importance of community, since individuals must realize that they are not the only ones drawing from that resource base. And so income, and consumption, must be kept at sustainable levels. We argue that they must be within the limits imposed by the long-term availability of the resource base for the entire ecological community. That means that absolute scarcity plays a role in shaping the conditions under which allocation takes place. The market may still be the principal allocator of most resources, but the amount of each resource to be allocated becomes a community rather than a market decision. The good life for the individual cannot be bought at the expense of the community. The rational egoistic individual must be subordinated and the "person-in-community" elevated.[20]

Such an approach requires a more careful definition of community so as to focus both political and economic attention in the right place. In the typical analyses, community is something larger than the individual, but it is not necessarily identical with the nation-state. Daly and Cobb put some dimensions on this with the claim that community means that "membership in a society contributes to self identification."[21] They also contend that the kind of community they envision would have three other requirements: members participate extensively in decisions, the society is responsible for its members, and there is respect for diverse individuality.[22]

In order to enact our vision of the good life and the common good, we believe that even more has to be said about the character of community. As we argued earlier in this chapter, an inclusive community must expand its membership in order to represent the interests of the future and nature. And there must be mechanisms available to focus the power of the extended community in its decision making. We have contended that even rational egoism, the pursuit of self-interest by the individual actor in the economic system, would have different outcomes if the community reshaped the individual's definition of self-interest. Now we argue for something more than that. We believe that in the community we envision, the individual *will* act for communal well-being, both in the shape of communal economic and political goals and in individual economic decision making. For example, prior to the 1980s there was consistent evidence in support of this in the United States when people voted to tax themselves to provide various educational and social services. Although it certainly did not characterize all of our behavior, there was a clear recognition that the common good was important and that it existed beyond narrowly defined self-interest.

Daly and Cobb's approach to community seems to come to rest on stewardship. We are not as confident about the effectiveness of that in driving us to a sustainable economy and ecology. We worry that their notion of "person-in-community" continues to be anthropocentric, and even if it begins to take account of absolute scarcity it will still focus on the economy as using resources for human purposes. For us, as we have said, there must be a way for the emerging communities to include future generations and nature. While they emphasize "person-in-community," we want to incorporate that as a part of "nature-in-community." Decisions that seem appropriate for the anthropocentric community might not be so for the naturocentric one. This is consistent with the four criteria that Daly and Cobb have proposed. For example, membership in the community would move nature from "object" to "subject," and for humans, at least, that is part of the process of self-identification. Taking responsibility for its members and respecting their diversity also does not seem out of line for a community that includes the future and the natural order. The most difficult task would seem to be providing for participation by its members in the decision-making process. It is not anthropocentric to recognize that in the real world decision making is a peculiarly human activity. It will be the current generation of human beings who effectively make the decisions. That being the case, to use the words of Dr. Seuss, "Who will speak for the trees?"[23] A truly ecological community requires that the decisions reflect the best interests of all the constituent parts, not just contemporary humans.

Certainly in our current U.S. society such communities are not prevalent. We have large centralized organizations that are deciding what and how much to produce and are spending large sums of advertising money to convince us that their choices mirror our own. The lack of competition, and the deleterious effects that lack has on the kinds of goods and services that are available and on their quantity and quality, is a reality for our society. Often both the consumption and the production of products generate wastes that damage our health and the long-term viability of our environment. The organizations that dominate our economic life have only their own well-being, power, and profit as goals, and without strong competitive forces, there is nothing to turn their interests in ways that consistently coincide with those of the consumer. They want to capture for themselves the exclusive right to define the good life. And there is certainly nothing built into their goals or the system to ensure the preservation of ecological balance. It is not much different from having a central planning authority; it is probably marginally more efficient but clearly less interested in social welfare.

We need to be careful, however, about defining the possible in terms of the current reality of our society and drawing the conclusion that such communities cannot exist. American Indian tribes, much of tribal Africa, and indigenous populations in the Amazon rain forest all have long histories of living in balance with nature, of forming effective human and natural communities that establish long-term ecological and economic sustainability. For them the good life cannot be conceived of independently of the common good. It is modern industrial societies—with their focus on the use of fossil fuels, ever-growing consumption, and human population growth—that have disrupted the balance. But we can't go back in time to undo the damage. We must begin where we are and see whether our own society, with its extant technology and its rampant industrialization, can be restructured into ecological communities that include nature and restore long-term balance.

In many ways our political and economic behavior in recent years has moved us in the opposite direction, toward an even more narrowly defined self-interested individualism. But it is curious that in defense of "individual" rights against an "ever encroaching" government, many have banded together in conservative coalitions, fundamentalist religious groups, cults, and paramilitary militia organizations. In other words, even "individualism" must be defined and lived out in community; communities and individuals do shape each others' values and behavior. So the task is not one of determining whether a community-based ethic is possible, but rather one of encouraging the revitalization of old communities and the formation of new ones with healthier sets of goals shaped by the language of the ecological trinity and driven to seek out the long-term common good.

Any sustainable vision of the good life can be enacted only within communities that are holistic and inclusive. In reality, we all belong to collections of overlapping communities, many of which emphasize social well-being. We need to look, then, at those facets of communities that emphasize their nonindividual character. What follows are modest suggestions that put forward the possibility that some of these communities/organizations might help to implement "person-and-nature-in-community."

We have contended at several points that the church is one organization that can play a role in addressing this situation. U.S. churches have a long history of providing resources that allow the powerless to begin to redress their economic disadvantage. For many, the largest problems associated with the distorted distribution of economic power are those that make it difficult for individual poor consumers to get the products they want and need from large corporations. However inappropriately, the good life has been defined, but it is not attainable. Those at the bottom of the income distribution represent such a small dollar value of demand for products that their needs are met by the system only imperfectly if at all. But it is possible to enhance the purchasing power of poor individuals by combining that power in cooperative structures. Churches have often provided the office and storage space that enable poor people's cooperatives to work effectively.

While churches themselves have not had a comparable history in the environmental arena, we believe that a similar approach to the use of cooperative buying power can also be used to create pressure for the environmentally safe production of environmentally safe products. In fact, as we have argued earlier, environmental problems are part of a continuum caused by patterns of exploitation and oppression. Those with power can insulate themselves to some extent from the ecological impacts of their economic activity. The powerless, on the other hand, not only must suffer the economic degradation of being on the wrong end of the power distribution, but also cannot escape the deleterious environmental side effects.

The issue of entrenched economic power needs to be addressed in other ways as well. Finding ways to enhance competitiveness and prevent the possibility of future concentration and accumulation can help dramatically in the implementation of an ecological vision. Political power can be organized and used to elect officials who interpret antitrust, antimonopoly legislation more strictly and therefore reduce concentration by preventing mergers and acquisitions. Endowments and pension funds can play a role here as well, by consistently using proxies to vote against corporate mergers. Once again, it is easy to see the continuum of exploitation at work here. Mergers in the 1980s and 1990s in the United States have led to successive waves of corporate downsizing and thus increased economic marginalization. At the same time, the increased size, and power, of corporate businesses insulates them from both the economic and the ecological consequences of their actions. Churches are among the organizations that can help bring pressure to bear to interpret and enforce the existing laws in different ways and thus change the existing distribution and use of economic power.

Finally, the income distribution issue is one that ought to be at the center of the church agenda. The organized economic and social power of the church can certainly be used to help those at the bottom to confront and bring about change in their condition. The economic system ought not to be organized in such a way that it engenders poverty, economic insecurity, and ecological damage. Those conditions should be unacceptable, whatever our definitions of the good life and the common good. The current economic reality, even after a long period of very strong economic growth, is increased misery for those at the bottom, and no real improvement for those in the lower middle. We often forget that there are environmental consequences attached to the income distribution as well. As we noted above, for example, the poor have a much harder time escaping or protecting themselves from environmental decay; they are often victims of environmental racism. But poverty also severely limits your ability to have adequate sewage treatment, to afford efficient heating systems, to adequately insulate your home, to maintain a car's pollution control systems, to hire trash collection services that recycle, or to educate your children about the environment. All of those things generate increased likelihood of widespread environmental degradation.

The church is not by any means the only organization that can help to create and implement change. It should focus on making common cause with others that recognize the environmental impacts of powerlessness. Environmental organizations have long been working toward an end to environmental degradation. Many of these have been very effective in building within their organization a sense of partnership with nature. As we argued earlier in this chapter, however, they have not been particularly effective at extending that partnership in ways that build a true ecological community. Environmental elitism and eco-terrorism may be effective ploys for solving particular problems, but they do not build the kind of inclusive community that is necessary to change the institutional arrangements so that degradation does not occur in the first place. We suggested earlier that a partnership between the logging workers and the environmentalists in the Pacific Northwest would help in building a long-term solution to the problem of rain forest and habitat destruction. Both sides in that dispute have a mutual interest in sustainability. They need to learn from each other how to broaden their individual notions of what that means. Building the good life for nonhuman species and environmentalists at the expense of workers is no more acceptable than its alternative. In more general terms, environmentalists cannot focus their attention only on protecting the environment when that protection has economic impacts on the human part of the community. Mutuality and reciprocity argue for solutions that are holistic, restoring the balance with nature while at the same time preserving long-run economic security, and protecting against short-run economic instability.

The argument also applies to organizations whose principal focus would seem to be on issues of economic security. For example, labor unions that fight environmental protection that costs jobs must find ways to recognize that long-term ecological security is in everyone's interests, and they must convince their members of that fact; it is neither impractical nor impossible. That also means that they must work hard to support the restoration of ecological integrity while minimizing the impact of the short-term economic insecurity suffered by workers. In the pure production sphere, Japanese quality-circle worker-management interaction has shown that greater efficiency, lower cost, and more-imaginative solutions arise from cooperative rather than antagonistic relationships among the participants in a process. The same should be true if the objective is the sustainability of economic and ecological security. Whatever our private interests, we are all members of an ecological community. At the highest level, boards of directors set corporate policy; that policy must be informed by inputs from labor and from environmental interests.

Our lack of communal values in economic matters and our highly individualized concept of the good life give us a corporate economic culture that often argues hard for market solutions for everyone else and market protection for themselves. But whether market-oriented or not, their vision of the common good is one that is based on pure self-interest, with no controlling community value system or ethic. The power to control the economy resides within that culture and it is there that the production and resource use decisions are being made. And remember, those decisions are among the most potent forces driving environmental degradation. Whatever we might do in an organizational sense to implement the ecological trinity of mutuality, connectedness, and community has to begin with diffusing the concentration of power that already exists.

The traditional economists' approach to diffusing power, redistributing the results of economic activity, is not being vigorously applied in today's political climate. But even in the late 1960s and early 1970s, while there was some progress at reducing poverty via redistribution, there was not much progress at changing the conditions that engender poverty. Those conditions are created by a system that claims to base rewards on productivity but actually bases them on economic power. The rhetoric of the system claims that those who are poor make only very small economic contributions to the society and therefore receive only small rewards. That claim would be more palatable if the very large rewards received by those at the top of the distribution could be traced to personal productive contributions. Unfortunately it is much more often power and wealth, not productivity, that "justifies" those large incomes. People in the top management positions in large corporations can control the compensation systems to ensure themselves large incomes whether or not the corporation does well. Even when they lose their positions, "golden parachutes" provide effective protection against the exigencies of poverty. In addition, people with large stocks of accumulated wealth, often inherited, can manipulate the system so that their wealth generates even more income and thus create the possibility for more accumulation. Stock options and capital gains are often the reward for being rich and powerful, not for being personally productive. Those without power are systematically excluded from that kind of reward. And since the ecological system itself, nature, has neither ownership nor voice, it is among the most powerless elements in the new community we advocate.

Organizations interested in redirecting power and restoring balance could seriously "up the ante" on exclusion. The church, environmental groups, labor unions, and other organizations have the muscle to put together such a move; the victims have the knowledge about the most appropriate targets. Corporations that won't bargain in good faith, that generate waste products without regard for the damage they cause, that use resources profligately, that eliminate jobs without cause, might all change their behavior if there were organized boycotts of the products and services they offer. The ingredient that is missing is the commonality of purpose that draws all of those organizations into a common bond. Recognizing the necessity of maintaining ecological integrity in all of our long-term behavior and restoring the balance between nature and human agency could provide that purpose.

A real reconfiguration of the good life and a connected service of the common good requires assets and commitment. We cannot solve problems of poverty just by calling for fair employment practices, and we cannot end environmental degradation by proclaiming the sanctity of nature. Better general and vocational education, on-the-job training, and quality child care are all necessities for a concerted attack on the sources of poverty; education, sacrifice, and changed consumption habits are needed to end environmental degradation. Each of those outcomes can flow only from new and changed institutional arrangements. Many existing organizations, if committed to a new type of community, have the facilities and the human resources to begin to bring that about. They can also pull together political power to support new legislation that provides funding and creates new institutions to make such programs a reality. The new values and the new institutions must grow up together.

Obviously, we think society needs to bring about change in all of these areas. Unfortunately, in recent years our society has often done the wrong things. Many of the issues we consider important have been the focus of *de-legislative* and *de-policy* attention. At one level, deregulating the U.S. economy has appeared to be an appropriate step. Its ostensible goal has been to free up the economic decision-making process so as to reduce its inefficiency and thereby improve everyone's level of well-being. But the potential positive impact of deregulation has often been overwhelmed by greed. The desire for more power and more economic control coupled with a hands-off government has led to a wave of mergers and acquisitions that have greatly increased the concentration of economic power in the society. The consequences of that have included substantial misuse of society's resources. Associated tax and spending policies, supposedly designed to raise productivity and generate a trickle-down improvement in overall economic welfare, have instead created a "gush up" of staggering growth in the incomes of the very richest members of society. The lack of a perichoretic vision and an extraordinarily narrow vision of the common good have allowed all of these factors to accelerate the pace of environmental degradation. If it is viewed as an experiment in enhancing societal well-being, the conservative retrenchment of the 1980s must be seen as a failure; subsequent federal policy by the new right in the 1990s has not improved things: productivity growth has been abysmal in recent years—from 1950 to 1974, output per worker grew by 86 percent; from 1975 to 1994 it grew by only 25 percent;[24] in addition, investment is far too low and it is not growing very rapidly; the conditions of those living in poverty are worse than they were in the late 1970s; the median real family income has barely improved, growing by less than 1 percent from 1973 to 1993.[25]

The Congress in 1995–96 has been threatening to continue all of those negative social policies and to dismantle most of the environmental protection legislation and structure as well.

Once again, the political power of many organizations, including the church, can be used in a consistent way to support the emergence of a social policy that puts the *welfare* of human beings and the environment, persons-and-nature-in-community, ahead of the *wants* of corporate beings. The creation of a new community is essential, but so are the institutional arrangements for implementing the goals of that new community. It will take a long time, but we must demand the creation of humane social and environmental policies in which pursuit of the good life does not overburden the bottom of the income distribution in order to provide benefits to the top. Such policies should see the protection of nature as intrinsically valuable and should recognize that the future is just as important as the present.

U.S. society and the global community have acted as though reality were a set of autistic adventures rather than a web of mutually interconnected and supporting systems. If we cannot overcome that view of reality then we are likely to be condemned to the fate envisioned by an American Indian writer, "when the last tree has been felled, and when the last river has been seized, only then will we finally realize that we cannot eat money."[26] Material production and consumption may have become enormous, the market may have dominated decision making, and individualism may have been pervasive, but all of that will be meaningless if nature is destroyed in the process. Our material conception of the good life will be quite empty if there is nowhere to live it. In the ultimate autistic act we will have ended what some affirm God began.

·NOTES·

1. The Origins of Environmental Degradation

1. Beverly W. Harrison, "The Power of Anger in the Work of Love: Christian Ethics for Women and Other Strangers," *Union Seminary Quarterly Review* xxxvi (1981): 49.

2. Lester R. Brown et al., *State of the World 1994* (New York: W. W. Norton & Company, 1994), 10.

3. Ibid., 11.

4. Lester R. Brown et al., *State of the World 1991* (New York: W.W. Norton, 1991), 7.

5. World Resources Institute, *World Resources 1994–95* (New York: Oxford University Press, 1994), 182.

6. Michael P. Todaro, *Economic Development in the Third World* (White Plains, N.Y.: Longman, 1985), 181.

7. Ohio Environmental Council, *Environmental Injustice in Ohio: A Work in Progress* (Columbus: Ohio Environmental Council, 1997), 20.

8. Ibid., 26.

9. Tom Tietenberg, *Environmental and Natural Resource Economics* (New York: HarperCollins, 1992), 21–35.

10. Michael Jacobs, *The Green Economy* (London: Pluto Press, 1991), 58–61.

11. Steven Lewis Yaffee, *The Wisdom of the Spotted Owl* (Washington, D.C.: Island Press, 1994), 6.

12. Ibid., 250.

13. Karen Baker-Fletcher and Garth Kasimu Baker-Fletcher, *My Sister, My Brother: Womanist and Xodus God-talk* (Maryknoll, N.Y.: Orbis Books, 1997), 39.

14. Rosemary Radford Ruether, *Gaia and God* (San Francisco: HarperSanFrancisco, 1992), 207.

15. Jürgen Moltmann, *The Crucified God: The Cross of Christ as the Foundation and Criticism of Christian Theology* (New York: Harper & Row, 1974), 329 ff.

16. Emilie M. Townes, *In a Blaze of Glory: A Womanist Spirituality as Social Witness* (Nashville: Abingdon Press, 1995), 55.

17. Ibid., 58.

18. Robert D. Bullard, *Dumping in Dixie* (Boulder, Colo.: Westview Press, 1994), 98.

19. Sallie McFague, *Models of God: Theology for an Ecological, Nuclear Age* (Philadelphia: Fortress Press, 1987), 15.

20. John Maynard Keynes, *The General Theory of Employment Interest and Money* (New York: Harcourt, Brace & World, 1936), 383.

21. Jürgen Moltmann, *God in Creation: A New Theology of Creation and the Spirit of God* (San Francisco: HarperSanFrancisco, 1991), 2.

22. Paul Santmire, *The Travail of Nature: The Ambiguous Ecological Promise of Christian Theology* (Philadelphia: Fortress Press, 1985).

23. Moltmann, *God in Creation*, 29.

24. Mark A. Lutz, "Centering Social Economics on Human Dignity," *Review of Social Economy* 53, no. 2 (1995): 171–92.

25. Ibid., 173.

26. Ibid., 189–90.

27. Ibid., 177–78.

28. The World Bank, *World Development Report 1996* (New York: Oxford University Press, 1996), 188–89.

29. Alice Walker, *Living by the Word* (San Diego: Harcourt, Brace, Jovanovich, 1988), 140.

30. Alice Walker, *The Color Purple* (New York: Washington Square Press, 1982), 178.

31. Baker-Fletcher, *My Sister, My Brother*, 136.

2. Individualism and Community in Economics and Theology

1. McFague, *Models of God*, 3.

2. Sallie McFague, *Super, Natural Christians: How We Should Love Nature* (Minneapolis: Fortress Press, 1997), 9.

3. Walker, *Living by the Word*, 147.

4. Ibid., 142.

5. Baker-Fletcher, *My Sister, My Brother*, 39–40.

6. Denis Edwards, *Jesus the Wisdom of God: An Ecological Theology* (Maryknoll, N.Y.: Orbis Books, 1995), 2.

7. Santmire, *The Travail of Nature*.

8. Jay B. McDaniel, *Of God and Pelicans: A Theology of Reverence for Life* (Louisville: Westminster/John Knox Press, 1989), 10.

9. Moltmann, *God in Creation*, XI.

10. Herman E. Daly, "A Biblical Economic Principle and the Steady-State Economy," in *Covenant for a New Creation*, ed. Carol S. Robb and Carl J. Casebolt (Maryknoll, N.Y.: Orbis Books, 1991), 47–48.

11. Baker-Fletcher, *My Sister, My Brother*, 189.

12. Ibid., 30.

13. Ibid., 180.

14. John F. Haught, "Religious and Cosmic Homelessness: Some Environmental

Implications," in *Liberating Life: Contemporary Approaches to Ecological Theology,* ed. Charles Birch, William Eakin, and Jay B. McDaniel (Maryknoll, N.Y.: Orbis Books, 1990), 163.

15. Paulo Freire, *Pedagogy of the Oppressed* (New York: Continuum, 1992).

16. Max Weber, *The Protestant Ethic and the Spirit of Capitalism* (New York: Charles Scribner's Sons, 1958), 37.

17. Leonardo Boff, *Ecology and Liberation* (Maryknoll, N.Y.: Orbis Books, 1995), 7.

18. Baker-Fletcher, *My Sister, My Brother,* 179.

19. Moltmann, *God in Creation,* 47.

20. Ibid., 259.

21. Jay B. McDaniel, *With Roots and Wings: Christianity in an Age of Ecology and Dialogue* (Maryknoll, N.Y.: Orbis Books, 1995), 3.

22. Paul G. King, Kent Maynard, and David O. Woodyard, *Risking Liberation* (Atlanta: John Knox Press, 1988), 61.

23. Chung Hyun Kyung, "Ecology, Feminism, and African and Asian Spirituality: Toward a Spirituality of Eco-Feminism," in *Ecotheology: Voices from South and North,* ed. David G. Hallman (Maryknoll, N.Y.: Orbis Books, 1994), 177.

24. Gustavo Gutiérrez, *A Theology of Liberation* (Maryknoll, N.Y.: Orbis Books, 1973), 146.

25. Ibid.

26. Ibid., 159.

27. McDaniel, *Of God and Pelicans,* 128.

28. Moltmann, *God in Creation,* 287.

29. Ibid.

30. Ibid., 279.

31. Ibid.

32. Joseph A. Schumpeter, *The Theory of Economic Development* (London: Oxford University Press, 1978).

33. Paul G. King and Daniel A. Underwood, "Sustainability, Innovation, and Development," paper presented to the annual meeting of the Association for Evolutionary Economics, Washington, D.C., January 6–8, 1995, 12.

34. Herman E. Daly, *Steady-State Economics,* 2d ed. (Washington, D.C.: Island Press, 1991).

35. Ibid., 50–75.

36. Ibid., 56–61.

37. Kenneth E. Boulding, *The Meaning of the Twentieth Century* (New York: Harper & Row, 1964), 135–36.

38. Daly, *Steady-State Economics,* 60.

39. Ibid., 61–68.

40. Ibid., 61.

41. Ibid., 64.

3. Economics and the Common Good

1. Brown et al., *State of the World 1991,* 3.

2. Ibid., 4.

3. Ibid., 5.

4. Ibid.

5. Ibid., 6.

6. Harold H. Oliver, "The Neglect and Recovery of Nature in Twentieth Century Protestant Thought," in *Journal of the American Academy of Religion* 60, no. 3 (fall 1992): 379.

7. Ibid., 381.

8. Ibid., 382–83.

9. Kenneth E. Boulding, "The Economics of the Coming Spaceship Earth," in *Environmental Quality in a Growing Economy,* ed. Henry Jarrett (Baltimore: Johns Hopkins University Press, 1966).

10. See Tietenberg, *Environmental and Natural Resource Economics,* 28.

11. Herman E. Daly, "Elements of Environmental Macroeconomics," in *Ecological Economics,* ed. Robert Costanza (New York: Columbia University Press, 1991), 39–44.

12. Ibid., 37–38.

13. See Dennis P. McCann, "Redeeming the 'City of Pigs': Catholic Principles for Welfare Justice," in *Catholic Social Teaching and the U.S. Economy,* ed. John W. Houck and Oliver F. Williams (Washington, D.C.: University Press of America, 1984), 193–95.

14. For example, see Harold Hotelling, "The Economics of Exhaustible Resources," *Journal of Political Economy* 39 (1931): 137–75.

15. Daly, "Elements of Environmental Macroeconomics," 44.

16. Cutler J. Cleveland, "Natural Resource Scarcity and Economic Growth Revisited: Economic and Biophysical Perspectives," in *Ecological Economics,* ed. Costanza, 293–94.

17. M. Douglas Meeks, *God the Economist* (Minneapolis: Fortress Press, 1989), 1.

18. John R. Earle, Dean D. Knudsen, and Donald W. Shriver Jr., *Spindles and Spires* (Atlanta: John Knox Press, 1976).

19. Meeks, *God the Economist,* xi.

20. McFague, *Models of God,* 43 ff.

21. Ibid., 47 ff.
22. Meeks, *God the Economist,* xi.
23. Herman E. Daly and John B. Cobb Jr., *For the Common Good* (Boston: Beacon Press, 1990), 159.
24. Ibid., 161.
25. James Weaver and Kenneth Jameson, *Economic Development: Competing Paradigms* (Washington, D.C.: University Press of America, 1981), 7–10.
26. United Nations Development Program, *Human Development Report 1994* (New York: Oxford University Press, 1994), 129.
27. *Economic Report of the President* (Washington, D.C.: U.S. Government Printing Office, 1997), 302.
28. "American Living Standards: Running to Stand Still," *The Economist,* November 10, 1990, 19–22.
29. William Ryan, *Equality* (New York: Vintage Books, 1981), 14.

4. Redirecting the Social System

1. Catharina J. M. Halkes, *New Creation* (Louisville: Westminster/John Knox Press, 1991), 97.
2. Ibid., 98.
3. Michael Novak, "A Theology of the Corporation," in *The Corporation: A Theological Inquiry,* ed. Michael Novak and John W. Cooper (Washington, D.C.: American Enterprise Institute, 1981), 203.
4. Alexander J. McKelway, *The Freedom of God and Human Liberation* (Philadelphia: Trinity Press International, 1990).
5. Ibid., 10 ff.
6. Sallie McFague, *The Body of God* (Minneapolis: Fortress Press, 1993), vii.
7. Moltmann, *God in Creation,* 318.
8. Pablo Richard, "Liberation Theology: Theology of the South," in *ENLIO: The Monthly Magazine of Central America* (June 1993): 32.
9. John Eagleson and Philip Scharper, eds., *Puebla and Beyond: Documentary and Commentary* (Maryknoll, N.Y.: Orbis Books, 1979).
10. Frances Moore Lappe and J. Baird Callicott, "Individual and Community in Society and Nature," in *Religion and Economic Justice,* ed. Michael Zweig (Philadelphia: Temple University Press, 1991), 47.
11. Ibid.
12. Michael Zweig, "Economics and Liberation Theology," in *Religion and Economic Justice,* ed. Zweig, 8.

13. Samuel Bowles and Herbert Gintis, "The Economy Produces People," in *Religion and Economic Justice,* ed. Zweig, 226.

14. Ibid., 227.

15. Lappe and Callicott, "Individual and Community in Society and Nature," 249.

16. Ibid.

17. Meeks, *God the Economist,* xi.

18. Anna Case-Winters, *God's Power* (Louisville: Westminster/John Knox Press, 1990), 19.

19. McFague, *Models of God.*

20. Gustavo Gutiérrez, *The God of Life* (Maryknoll, N.Y.: Orbis Books, 1991).

21. Gutiérrez, *A Theology of Liberation,* 189.

22. Ibid., 194.

23. Ibid., 195.

24. Ibid., 204–5.

25. Gutiérrez, *The God of Life,* xii–xiii.

26. Ibid., xiii.

27. Ibid., 6.

28. Ibid., 75.

29. Ibid.

30. Ibid., 78.

31. Ibid., 81.

32. Baker-Fletcher, *My Sister, My Brother,* 39.

33. Ingemar Hedstrom, "Latin America and the Need for a Life-Liberating Theology," in *Liberating Life,* ed. Birch, Eakin, and McDaniel, 116–20.

34. McFague, *Models of God,* 35.

35. Baker-Fletcher, *My Sister, My Brother,* 85.

36. Robert Costanza, Herman E. Daly, and Joy A. Bartholomew, "Goals, Agenda and Policy Recommendations for Ecological Economics," in *Ecological Economics,* ed. Costanza, 2–3.

37. Ibid., 3.

5. Prelude to a New Order

1. William T. Utter, *Granville: The Story of an Ohio Village* (Granville, Ohio: Granville Historical Society, 1956), 57.

2. Ibid.

3. Ibid., 56.

4. Walter Brueggemann, *Prophetic Imagination* (Philadelphia: Fortress Press, 1978), 12.

5. Robert N. Bellah et al., *Habits of the Heart* (Berkeley: University of California Press, 1985), 27.

6. Max Oelschlaeger, *Caring for Creation* (New Haven, Conn.: Yale University Press, 1994), 54.

7. King, Maynard, and Woodyard, *Risking Liberation,* 100.

8. Bellah et al., *Habits of the Heart,* 336.

9. Adam Smith, *The Wealth of Nations* (New York: The Modern Library, 1937), 423.

10. Meeks, *God the Economist,* 29.

11. Oelschlaeger, *Caring for Creation,* 49.

12. Ibid.

13. Ibid., 5.

14. Peter Berger, *The Sacred Canopy* (New York: Doubleday, 1969), 39.

15. Ibid., 32.

16. Ibid., 33.

17. Oelschlaeger, *Caring for Creation,* 48.

18. Bruce Lincoln, as quoted in Oelschlager, *Caring for Creation,* 61.

19. Brueggemann, *Prophetic Imagination,* 28.

20. Peter L. Berger and Richard John Neuhaus, *To Empower People* (Washington, D.C.: American Enterprise Institute, 1977), 2.

21. Richard C. Austin, *Hope for the Land* (Atlanta: John Knox Press, 1988), 234.

22. Ibid., 106.

23. John Howard Yoder, *The Politics of Jesus* (Grand Rapids, Mich.: Eerdmans, 1972), 36.

24. Sean McDonagh, *Passion for the Earth* (Maryknoll, N.Y.: Orbis Books, 1994), 142.

25. Ibid.

26. Ibid., 143.

27. Edwards, *Jesus the Wisdom of God,* 19.

28. Ibid., 30.

29. Ibid., 33.

30. Baker-Fletcher, *My Sister, My Brother,* 84.

31. McFague, *Models of God,* 139.

32. James H. Cone, *Black Theology of Liberation* (Maryknoll, N.Y.: Orbis Books, 1986), 104.

33. McFague, *Super, Natural Christians,* 174.

34. Austin, *Hope for the Land,* 208.

35. John Cobb Jr., *Sustaining the Common Good* (Cleveland: The Pilgrim Press, 1994), viii.

6. Implementing the New Order

1. Alice Walker, as quoted in McFague, *Super, Natural Christians,* 44.

2. Stephen L. Carter, *The Culture of Disbelief* (New Haven, Conn.: Yale University Press, 1994).

3. Wolfhart Pannenberg, *Christian Spirituality* (Philadelphia: Westminster Press, 1983), 35.

4. Brueggemann, *Prophetic Imagination,* 12.

5. Oelschlaeger, *Caring for Creation,* 220.

6. Stanley Hauerwas, *The Peaceable Kingdom* (Notre Dame, Ind.: University of Notre Dame Press, 1983), 99 ff.

7. Ibid., 103.

8. Pannenberg, *Christian Spirituality,* 35.

9. Walker, *The Color Purple,* 167.

10. Brueggemann, *Prophetic Imagination,* 11 ff.

11. Oelschlaeger, *Caring for Creation,* 220.

12. King, Maynard, and Woodyard, *Risking Liberation,* 169.

13. Ibid., 170.

14. Charles Cummings, "Friend of the Earth, Fruit of the Vine," in *Embracing the Earth,* ed. Albert LaChance and John E. Carroll (Maryknoll, N.Y.: Orbis Books, 1994), 159.

15. Lappe and Callicott, "Individual and Community in Society and Nature," 247.

16. McDaniel, *With Roots and Wings,* 171.

17. Bellah et al., *Habits of the Heart,* viii.

18. Daly and Cobb, *For the Common Good,* 138.

19. Ibid., 70.

20. Ibid., 159–75.

21. Ibid., 172.

22. Ibid., 72.

23. Dr. Seuss, *The Lorax* (New York: Random House, 1971).

24. *Economic Report of the President* (Washington, D.C.: U.S. Government Printing Office, 1995), 328.

25. Ibid., 310.

26. An unnamed author, as quoted in Boff, *Ecology and Liberation,* 35.

·INDEX·